T0168785

An Analysis of the Veterans Equitable Resource Allocation (VERA) System

Jeffrey Wasserman
Jeanne Ringel
Barbara Wynn
Jack Zwanziger
Karen Ricci
Sydne Newberry
Barbara Genovese
Michael Schoenbaum

Prepared for the Department of Veteran Affairs

National Defense Research Institute | **RAND** Health

RAND

Approved for public release; distribution unlimited

The research described in this report was sponsored by the Department of Veterans Affairs (DVA). The research was conducted jointly by RAND Health's Center for Military Health Policy Research and the Forces and Resources Policy Center of the National Defense Research Institute, a federally funded research and development center supported by the OSD, the Joint Staff, the unified commands, and the defense agencies under Contract DASW01-01-C-0004.

Library of Congress Cataloging-in-Publication Data

An analysis of the Veterans Equitable Resource Allocation (VERA) system / Jeffrey
    Wasserman ... [et al.].
        p. cm.
        "MR-1419."
        Includes bibliographical references.
        ISBN 0-8330-3064-7
        1. Veterans—Health and hygiene—United States. 2. United States. Veterans
    Health Administration—Rules and practice. I. Wasserman, Jeffrey.

    UB357 .A748 2001
    362.1'086'97—dc21

                                                                            2001048390

RAND is a nonprofit institution that helps improve policy and decisionmaking through research and analysis. RAND® is a registered trademark. RAND's publications do not necessarily reflect the opinions or policies of its research sponsors.

Published 2001 by RAND
1700 Main Street, P.O. Box 2138, Santa Monica, CA 90407-2138
1200 South Hayes Street, Arlington, VA 22202-5050
201 North Craig Street, Suite 102, Pittsburgh, PA 15213
RAND URL: http://www.rand.org/
To order RAND documents or to obtain additional information, contact
Distribution Services: Telephone: (310) 451-7002; Fax: (310) 451-6915;
Email: order@rand.org

The Veterans Equitable Resource Allocation (VERA) system was instituted by the Veterans Health Administration (VHA)—the organization in the Department of Veterans Affairs (DVA) that is responsible for providing health care to veterans—in 1997. The system was designed to improve the allocation of the congressionally appropriated medical care budget to the 22 regional service networks that comprise the VA health system. In recent legislation (H.R. 4635), the U.S. Congress asked the DVA to conduct a study on whether VERA adequately meets the special needs of some veterans. In response to this legislation, the VHA asked RAND's National Defense Research Institute to undertake this study. Specifically, this study examines the degree to which VERA accounts for differences in the age and geographic location of facilities, their patient case mixes, and other factors. The study also examines cost issues associated with affiliations between VA facilities and academic medical centers. The findings and recommendations from the study are documented in this report.

Study findings should be of interest to VA personnel, Congress, and other policymakers—particularly those interested in health care for veterans. Health economists and policy planners may also have an interest in the findings.

This research was sponsored by the DVA and was carried out jointly by RAND Health's Center for Military Health Policy Research and the Forces and Resources Policy Center of the National Defense Research Institute. The latter is a federally funded research and development center sponsored by the Office of the Secretary of Defense, the Joint Staff, the unified commands, and the defense agencies.

CONTENTS

FIGURES

TABLES

BACKGROUND AND APPROACH

The Veterans Equitable Resource Allocation (VERA) system represents the most recent effort of the Veterans Health Administration (VHA) to implement a resource allocation system that is both equitable and efficient and that preserves, if not enhances, VHA's commitment to providing high-quality health care to the veteran population. Since April 1997, VERA has served as the basis for allocating the congressionally appropriated medical care budget of the Department of Veterans Affairs (DVA)—which currently stands in excess of $20 billion—to 22 regional Veterans Integrated Service Networks (VISNs). Reflecting the VHA's commitment to provide high-quality health care to the veteran population, the system was designed to reflect changes in the geographic distribution of veterans over time and regional differences in health care needs and the costs of providing care, by periodically adjusting the allocations. At the same time, the system was designed to be simple and to be responsive to the health care needs of the highest-priority veterans, that is, those with service-connected disabilities. Concerned that the system does not allocate resources in a manner that allows the VHA to focus its provision of health care services appropriately, Congress requested a study of the VERA system. This report describes the results of an analysis of the VERA system that was undertaken on behalf of the VHA.

The legislative language and subsequent scope of work developed by VHA specified three tasks:

- an assessment of the impact of the allocation of funds under the VERA formula on VISNs and subregions with older-than-average medical facilities; those with older or more disabled enrolled veterans; those undergoing major consolidation; and those in both rural and urban subregions with appointment backlogs and waiting periods

- an assessment of issues associated with the maintenance of direct affiliations between the DVA medical centers and university teaching and research hospitals

- an assessment of whether the VERA formula accounts for differences in weather conditions when calculating costs of construction and maintenance of health care facilities, and whether VISNs that experience harsh weather require more resources

In light of the project's short time frame, we used qualitative research techniques to address these issues. The data for the report were gathered from three sources. The first source of data consisted of government documents, including reports on earlier evaluations of VERA as well as various editions of the VERA Book, which is published annually by the DVA.

The second source of data consisted of the health services research literature from the past 15–20 years. We conducted extensive bibliographic searches of medical, economic, social sciences, and business literature databases using a set of keywords we developed for each task. Literature that covered both the VA and civilian systems was included.

Finally, our analysis relied heavily on a series of interviews conducted at a sample of VISNs and facilities. To address the issues related to affiliations between the DVA medical centers and academic medical centers, we also conducted a set of interviews with representatives of organizations and institutions that have a stake in academic medicine.

We recognize that a quantitative analysis of the available data would provide greater insight into the issues of interest. Thus, the report includes a plan for conducting such an analysis.

FINDINGS

The findings of our analysis are of two types. The first of those is the identification of factors that may influence the costs of, and access to, care within the Veterans Administration (VA) system. The second is how VERA currently adjusts for those effects.

Our findings suggest that health care delivery costs may be affected by the age, physical condition, and historical significance of a VISN's capital infrastructure. VERA does not currently adjust for these differences. We also find that VERA's current case-mix adjustment, designed for simplicity, may not adequately account for differences in the average health status of veterans across VISNs and appears to provide incentives to game the system. In contrast, the influence on costs and access to care of such factors as the number of facilities in an area, the breadth of services offered, rural vs. urban location, and weather extremes is less clear.

Our analysis of the effect of academic affiliations on patient care costs revealed that VERA accounts for the costs directly attributable to research and education. However, VERA makes no explicit adjustment for the potential effects that academic affiliation might have on other patient costs. Moreover, the distinction between education support funds and patient-care funds may be artificial, because residents provide patient-care services and affect productivity.

Finally, we want to emphasize that in spite of VERA's possible shortcomings, we note that VERA appears to be designed to meet its objectives of reallocating resources to match the geographic distribution of the veteran population more closely than did previous VA budget allocation systems. In addition, the overwhelming majority of interviewees indicated that VERA was preferable to previous systems in terms of its incentive structure, degree of fairness, and simplicity. We also wish to note that VERA undergoes refinement on a continuous basis. The present study represents the latest in a series of evaluations undertaken by external organizations since the system's inception less than five years ago. Moreover, work groups composed of representatives from the 22 VISNs constantly monitor various aspects of the system's operations and recommend modifications. VHA has implemented many of the recommended changes contained in both the external evaluators' reports as well as the work groups' memoranda.

IMPLICATIONS AND PROPOSED ANALYSIS

A number of critical issues emerged during the course of our study that we believe warrant additional consideration. We believe these issues can best be addressed through a quantitative analysis of various VA data sets. The results of this analysis could be translated immediately into changes in the ways VERA allocates resources to VISNs.

The factors we believe require additional analysis include the following:

- the health status of the population served—specifically, whether any of the proposed changes to the methodology used to determine case mix would better reflect costs;

- the intensity of the affiliation between individual VA medical facilities and teaching and/or research institutions;

- physical plant characteristics, including the age of the facility, its size relative to the population it serves, its historical significance (if any), its breadth of service, the number of facilities in the same area, and any special maintenance needs; and

- geographic price variation in nonlabor inputs (e.g., energy, food, medical supplies, and pharmaceuticals).

The recommended analysis will account for individual-, facility-, and VISN-level factors in its consideration of potential modifications to VERA. This analysis will provide critical information on possible VERA modifications. But ultimately, policymakers will need to decide whether any such modifications are consistent with VERA's goals and objectives.

Apart from our proposed analysis, we have several additional recommendations. First, a geographic adjustment to the means test that is used to determine a veteran's financial status should be considered with regard to eligibility for services. However, we are aware that a change in the eligibility measures is not within the purview of the DVA and would require congressional action. Second, we believe that the workload forecasting process can be improved by relying on more sophisticated methods. Improving the forecasting process would, in turn, increase the ability of VISN directors to manage their operations and potentially improve veterans' access to care.

Finally, our findings suggest that many factors influence the VA health care delivery system. The interactions among these factors necessitate policy analyses that account for the entire context in which the VA operates.

ACKNOWLEDGMENTS

We are extremely grateful for the valuable support that we received throughout this project from our Project Officer at the Veterans Health Administration (VHA), John Vecciarelli. We also appreciate the time and energy that several other VHA officials devoted to the project, including Jimmy A. Norris, Paul Kearns, and Bernadette Bradley. We are also indebted to the members of the VHA Steering Committee that was assembled to provide overall project guidance. Many Veterans Integrated Service Network (VISN) and facility directors, as well as members of their staffs, patiently responded to our questions during our interviews, and for this we are most grateful. We would like to thank Landon Donsbach for his assistance in preparing this manuscript and for providing general administrative support to the project. Finally, we have benefited greatly from the thoughtful comments provided by Susan D. Hosek, Peter D. Jacobson, and Judith R. Lave, who reviewed an earlier version of this report.

ACGME	Accreditation Council for Graduate Medical Education
ARC	Allocation Resource Center
CBOC	Community-Based Outpatient Clinic
COTH	College of Teaching Hospitals
DCG	Diagnostic Cost Group
DVA	Department of Veterans Affairs
FTE	Full-time equivalent
FY	Fiscal year
GAO	(U.S.) General Accounting Office
MCCF	Medical care cost fund
NDRI	National Defense Research Institute
NRM	Nonrecurring maintenance
PRP	Prorated Patient
RPM	Resource Planning and Management
RRC	Residency Review Committee
VA	Veterans Administration (DVA)
VAMC	Veterans Administration Medical Center(s)
VERA	Veterans Equitable Resource Allocation
VHA	Veterans Health Administration
VISN	Veterans Integrated Service Network

Chapter One

INTRODUCTION

The Veterans Equitable Resource Allocation (VERA) system represents the most recent effort of the Veterans Health Administration (VHA) to implement a resource allocation system that is both equitable and efficient and that preserves, if not enhances, VHA's commitment to providing high-quality health care to the veteran population.

Since April 1997, VERA has served as the basis for allocating the congressionally appropriated medical care budget of the Department of Veterans Affairs (DVA)—which currently stands in excess of $20 billion—to 22 regional Veterans Integrated Service Networks (VISNs). Underlying the allocation system is a series of objectives that includes the following:

1. Resource allocations to the VISNs must change over time to reflect changes in the geographic distribution of the veteran population;

2. Resource allocation decisions should reflect geographic differences in the costs of providing care and the health care needs of the veteran population; and

3. The system is carefully monitored, and periodic refinements are made to the allocation methodology when warranted.

Moreover, the architects of VERA sought to design an allocation system that is perceived to be equitable, understandable, and focused on ensuring that health care is delivered to the highest-priority veterans (i.e., those with service-connected disabilities, special health care needs, and/or low incomes).

Congress has expressed concerns that the VERA system has reallocated funds dramatically in the past few years and that the distribution may no longer cover the special needs of veterans equitably. The purpose of this report is to describe the results of an analysis of the VERA system that was undertaken by RAND's National Defense Research Institute (NDRI) on behalf of the VHA. VHA contracted with NDRI to examine specific aspects of the system in response to a recent congressional mandate (H.R. 4635) requiring the DVA to study "whether VERA may lead to a distribution of funds that does not cover the special needs of some veterans." The legislative language, and subsequent scope of work developed by VHA, specified three tasks:

- an assessment of the impact of the allocation of funds under the VERA formula on VISNs and subregions with older-than-average medical facilities; those with older or more disabled enrolled veterans; those undergoing major consolidation; and those in both rural and urban subregions with appointment backlogs and waiting periods;

- an assessment of issues associated with the maintenance of direct affiliations between the DVA medical centers and university teaching and research hospitals; and

- an assessment of whether the VERA formula accounts for differences in weather conditions when calculating cost of construction and maintenance of health care facilities and whether VISNs that experience harsh weather require more resources.

In light of the project's short time frame, we used qualitative research techniques—primarily reviews of the relevant literature and a series of interviews—to address the issues listed above. The precise data sources and methods used in our analysis are described in Chapter 2. However, we recognize that with additional time, greater insight into these issues can be generated through a quantitative analysis of the available data. Consequently, in Chapter 6, we present a plan for conducting such an analysis.

In the remainder of this chapter we present a description of VERA. This description is followed by a discussion of the incentives created by the system for VISN and facility directors.

DESCRIPTION OF THE VERA SYSTEM

As shown in Figure 1.1, VERA comprises two major components: General Purpose funds, which account for nearly 90 percent of the annual appropriation, and Specific Purpose funds.[1] General Purpose funds are used to cover the

---

[1] For a detailed description of VERA, see Department of Veterans Affairs, *Veterans Equitable Resource Allocation System 2001*, Washington, D.C.: Department of Veterans Affairs, March 2001.

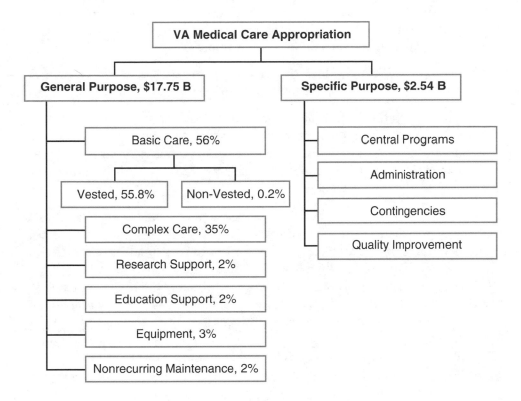

Figure 1.1—Components of VERA Funding

costs of patient care, research support, education support, equipment, and nonrecurring maintenance (NRM). The direct costs of research are provided in a separate appropriation and the direct costs of education are included as part of the Specific Purpose program. Specific Purpose funds are used to finance the costs associated with programs that are administered by VHA headquarters— including, for example, the provision of prosthetic devices, quality improvement initiatives, and database development—as well as headquarters' administrative expenses. A portion of the Specific Purpose funds is held in reserve to cover contingencies that may arise during the course of the fiscal year (FY), including potential shortages in funds allocated through VERA to the 22 VISNs.

Over 90 percent of the General Purpose funds are devoted to treating patients. Based on care needs, patients are classified into one of two categories: Basic Care and Complex Care. Basic Care patients are considered to be those patients who have relatively routine health care needs. They may require preventive, acute, and/or chronic health care services delivered in either an inpatient or ambulatory setting. Furthermore, VERA distinguishes between Vested and Non-Vested Basic Care Patients:

- Vested patients had either an inpatient stay or received a comprehensive health examination during the three-year period used to identify and classify patients for allocation purposes.

- Non-vested patients include individuals who have met neither of these criteria but who are occasional consumers of outpatient services.

Complex Care patients require substantial health care resources to treat chronic illnesses or disabling conditions over a long time frame. Many Complex Care patients are included in one of VHA's special emphasis programs (such as spinal cord injury, blind rehabilitation, post-traumatic stress disorder, and the like) or require long-term care.

VERA funds for treating Basic and Complex Care patients are allocated to VISNs based on "workload," which is essentially a measure of the number of patients treated, and a set of national prices. National prices, the amounts allocated annually per patient for treatment, are calculated for Basic Vested Care, Basic Non-Vested Care, and Complex Care Patients by taking the funds allocated for each of these categories and dividing by the forecasted national workload. For example, the Basic Vested Care price for FY 2001 was arrived at by dividing the $9.9 billion budget allocation for Basic Vested Care by a forecasted workload of 3.2 million to obtain a national price of $3,126 per case. The national prices for Basic Non-Vested and Complex Care in FY 2001 were $121 and $42,765, respectively. The allocation to a particular VISN for Basic Vested care is simply the product of the VISN's workload estimate and the national price, adjusted for geographic variation in labor costs.

In addition to covering the costs associated with patient care, VERA allocated over $1.5 billion to the VISNs in FY 2001 to support research, education, equipment purchases, and NRM expenses. Research support allocations to the networks for FY 2001 were based on the amount of research funded in FY 1999. Education support is allocated on the basis of the number of approved residents. In contrast, equipment and NRM funds are allocated strictly on the basis of workload. The Boeckh Index, which is published by Marshall & Swift/Boeckh, is used to adjust NRM for geographic differences in construction costs. Appendix A contains a description of the formulas used to allocate VERA funds in FY 2001.

UNDERSTANDING THE INCENTIVES CREATED BY VERA

VERA presents VISN directors and facility administrators with a complex set of incentives. As indicated above, patient care resources are allocated on a capitation basis, whereby VISNs receive a fixed amount of money for each patient. However, the denominator (number of patients) used to set the national prices is the number of expected patients, rather than, for example, the entire veteran population residing in the networks' service areas. Nevertheless, VERA provides a strong economic incentive to increase the number of cases treated while minimizing the costs per case by, for instance, shifting the delivery of care from inpatient to outpatient settings whenever possible and otherwise limiting the quantity of services delivered to patients.

However, unlike allocations governed by other government and private-sector capitation arrangements, the total allocation to VISNs is capped by the amount of the annual congressional appropriation. As a result, the VISNs compete for funds in what is essentially a zero-sum game. In other words, in a given year, the size of the pie remains fixed, with allocations to the individual VISNs being determined by their proportions of the total veteran workload. Thus, over time, if a particular VISN's workload increases at a faster rate than that of the other VISNs, it will receive a larger fraction of the total available funds. Additionally, if the growth rate of the total annual appropriation falls short of the growth in workload, then the amounts of resources allocated per patient will decrease over time.

In principle, the capitated nature of the system provides an economic incentive to minimize costs per case. This cost minimization can be achieved through a number of means. In general, care managers and providers can be expected to treat patients in the least costly setting possible and to avoid unnecessary tests, procedures, and medications. At the same time, VERA provides an incentive to enroll patients who can be expected to place few demands on the system and to avoid enrolling patients who are expected to be costly. However, for several reasons, the extent to which such enrollment manipulation actually occurs, if at all, is difficult to assess. First, how relatively healthy patients can be identified and recruited is unclear, although theoretically, managers could launch marketing campaigns and apply a "hard sell" to patients who demonstrate good overall health through, say, an initial exam. Second, given the VA's mission of serving veterans most in need of health care, it is unlikely, though certainly possible, that facility managers seeking to minimize costs in their own institutions would attempt to "dump" patients who prove to be costly on another facility within the VISN or on a facility located within another VISN. Ultimately, this question can be addressed by analyzing the relevant patient-level data sets.

Under the VERA system, per-patient allocations are based on only three case categories—Basic Vested, Basic Non-Vested, and Complex—in order to simplify the classification system. The allocations for each category differ substantially, ranging from $121 for Basic Non-Vested patients to $42,765 for Complex Care patients. The large disparity among per-patient allocations for the three case categories does leave open the possibility for managers to "game" the system somewhat, especially since the algorithms used to assign cases to categories include utilization as a factor. For example, in some cases, a patient with a condition that would ordinarily classify him or her as a Basic Vested patient could be classified as a Complex Care patient if his or her hospital stay were extended by one or two days. In addition, this relatively crude way of accounting for case mix could lead to systemwide inequities. This issue will be discussed further in Chapter 3.

It is important to note that the delivery of health care to veterans takes place within a larger context that both alters the incentives faced by health care administrators and providers and constrains their behavior. In fact, a complex interplay exists between VERA and a host of other factors that influence the cost, quantity, and quality of health care delivered to veterans. As illustrated in Figure 1.2, these factors include, but are certainly not limited to, the financial resources available, population shifts, historical infrastructure characteristics, quality improvement imperatives, the availability of non-VA sources of care, political considerations, general health care market forces, the VA's mission to provide health care of the highest possible quality, and government procedures and regulations. Moreover, in addition to the direct influence exerted by each of these factors, an untold number of indirect factors as well as interactions among the different factors influence patient care provided to veterans.

VERA plays a critical, yet in some respects limited, role in determining the resources available to treat patients. Other factors influencing patient care resources include the size of the annual congressional VHA appropriation, the amount of funds that facilities and VISNs are able to collect from third-party payers who cover veterans treated in VA facilities, and the ways in which resources are allocated by the VISNs to individual facilities. With respect to the latter consideration, recall that VERA is solely a mechanism for allocating the annual appropriation to the VISNs. Once such allocations are made, the VISN has enormous discretion when it comes to determining how funds should be allocated to facilities.[2] Consequently, care managers at the facility level may face very different economic incentives than do VISN directors.

VISN directors and facility administrators face a number of formidable constraints on their cost-minimizing behavior. For example, while VERA provides a clear-cut incentive for them to increase the number of enrolled veterans—often by opening community-based outpatient clinics (CBOCs)—capacity constraints and initiation costs may limit their ability to do so. Moreover, veterans groups,

---

[2] Here, it should be noted that, in response to early criticism of VERA, VHA has articulated a set of general principles that VISN directors are expected to abide by in making their allocation decisions.

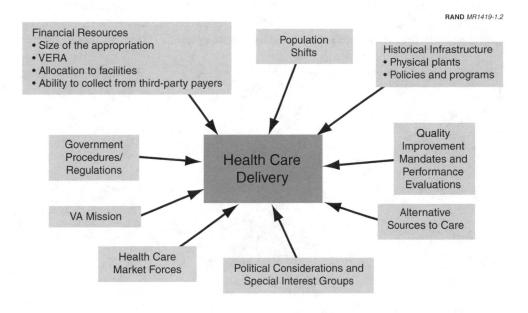

RAND *MR1419-1.2*

Figure 1.2—Influences on the VA Health Care System

local politicians, and other political considerations may limit their ability to close underused or inefficient facilities or even to consolidate particular services. Finally, VHA's performance measurement system—which, in addition to collecting information on a wide range of quality measures, also collects data related to access to care—helps to ensure that efforts aimed at improving efficiency do not end up compromising the quality of care delivered. However, at present, the financial incentives faced by VISN directors are not linked with quality standards.

The remainder of this report is organized into six chapters. In Chapter 2, we present a description of the data sources and methods used in our analysis. Chapter 3 is devoted to discussing the impact of VERA on older medical facilities, older and more disabled enrollees, service and facility consolidations, and backlogs and waiting times. Chapter 4 presents our assessment of how VERA has affected affiliations between DVA medical centers and university teaching and research hospitals. Chapter 5 reports the results of our analysis of the extent to which VERA accounts for differences in weather patterns across the VISNs and whether VISNs located in relatively harsh weather regions require more resources to deliver patient care. Chapter 6 presents a detailed plan for conducting a quantitative analysis of the issues raised in this report, which, in turn, would serve as a means for making further refinements to VERA. Finally, we present our conclusions in Chapter 7.

Chapter Two

DATA SOURCES AND METHODS

As we indicated in Chapter 1, our analysis relied primarily on three data sources:

1. data that were obtained primarily from government documents, including reports on earlier evaluations of VERA as well as all editions of the VERA book, which is published annually by the DVA

2. the health services research literature

3. a series of interviews conducted at a sample of VISNs and facilities

To address the issues related to direct affiliations between the DVA medical centers and university teaching and research hospitals, we also conducted a series of interviews with representatives of organizations and institutions that have a stake in academic medicine.

DOCUMENT AND LITERATURE REVIEWS

We reviewed all key documents and reports on the VERA system. These included the 1997–2001 VERA Books published by the Department of Veterans Affairs, two U.S. General Accounting Office (GAO) reports on VERA (GAO, 1997, 1998), an evaluation of various aspects of VERA conducted by Price Waterhouse LLP and The Lewin Group, Inc., (1998), and two studies conducted by a team of analysts from AMA Systems, Inc. and the Center for Naval Analysis Corporation (March 2000; July 2000). Taken together, these reports provided critical background information on the characteristics of VERA as well as a myriad of insights on the system's performance to date.

In addition to reviewing the reports listed above, we conducted an extensive bibliographic search using the following computerized data bases: Applied Science and Technology Index, Business Periodicals Index, EconLit, Social Science Index, Pais International, and MEDLINE on PUBMED. For each of the three major research tasks, we developed a set of keywords and searched each of the databases. Although the precise time frame for defining the searches varied somewhat, it typically covered 15–20 years.

Upon completing the on-line literature searches, we retrieved all promising articles and then searched the reference list contained in each to uncover citations that were not identified through the computerized search. Finally, we conducted a series of "forward searches" in which we attempted to identify articles that referenced any of the key articles that we identified through the initial bibliographic search.

VISN AND FACILITY INTERVIEWS

Our analysis relies heavily on the results of a set of interviews that we conducted at 13 of the 22 VISNs and 15 facilities (all VA Medical Centers, or VAMCs) located within those VISNs.[1] As few as 4 and as many as 11 VAMCs reside within each of the VISNs, with 7 being the average number. The number of VISNs and facilities visited was dictated largely by budgetary considerations. Moreover, in selecting the VISNs, we sought to include VISNs that benefited greatly under VERA, some that fared poorly, as well as some that fell in the middle, based on the changes in their budget allocations. We also included at least one VISN in each major geographic region (i.e., the Northeast, South, Midwest, and West). By including a number of VISNs located in the Northeast and South, we were able to investigate issues related to treating individuals who were geographically mobile (so-called "snowbirds"). Figure 2.1 depicts the VISNs included in the study.[2]

In selecting facilities for study, we took several factors into account. Again, budget considerations typically played a role in that we often (but not always) selected facilities located relatively close to the VISN office to minimize travel costs. Additionally, we selected some facilities that maintained strong affiliations with one or more teaching or research hospitals and some that had no such ties. We also included both urban and rural facilities in our sample. Once VISNs and facilities were selected, a member of the project team contacted the VISN and facility directors and explained the purpose and format of our intended visit. Staff from all VISNs and facilities that we contacted agreed to meet with us, and in a number of instances, they rearranged staff schedules to accommodate our travel plans. We recommended that the director and chief

---

[1] We visited one facility in each of nine VISNs, two facilities in each of three VISNs, and only the VISN office in the remaining VISN.

[2] VISNs in the Pacific Northwest and the Central States were not selected, primarily because of budgetary constraints and difficulty in consolidating travel itineraries.

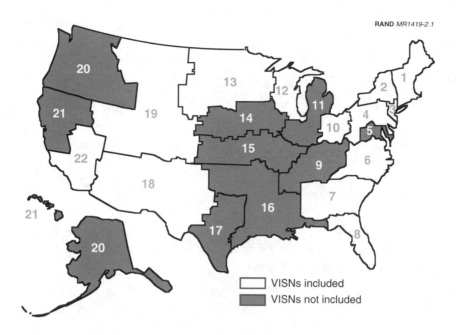

RAND *MR1419-2.1*

Figure 2.1—VISNs included in Interviews

financial officer be present, as well as any other management staff that the director believed should be included.

Most of the site visits were conducted in person. However, in those instances in which it was not possible to conduct face-to-face meetings, we interviewed representatives of the VISNs and facilities by phone. The interviews varied in length, but generally ran several hours. For the most part, two RAND staff members conducted the interviews.

In total, we met with 175 people across the 13 VISNs and 15 facilities. In all instances, we interviewed several people at each site. Generally, we spoke with the VISN or facility director and the chief financial officer. Often, we also spoke with compliance officers, resource allocation specialists, medical education directors, service chiefs, and care line/product line managers. At some VISNs and facilities, we met with one individual at a time, while at others we met with large groups of interviewees at once. We provided the interviewees with a strict confidentiality assurance, telling them that without their permission, we would neither cite them by name in our reports, nor would we provide any information that would allow readers to deduce an individual's identity without their permission. In addition, we promised not to share their comments with other interviewees or with any VHA headquarters officials. For these reasons, we have not included the detailed interviews in this report.

Interviewers used a semi-structured interview guide to organize note taking, ensure that all relevant topics were covered, and provide a consistent approach to data collection across interviewers and sites. The VISN and facility guides are included in Appendix B. The interviews covered a wide range of topics. General topics included the following:

- the demographic and health characteristics of the population served;

- the general physical and political environment within which the VISN or facility operates;

- the range of services offered and the characteristics of the facilities that provide them;

- the relationship between the VISN and its facilities, including how budget allocation decisions are made and how management conflicts are communicated and resolved;

- the impact of VERA on patient care; the financial health of the VISN/facility; the mix of services; the recruitment and retention of staff; quality improvement initiatives; and medical education and research;

- how VERA compares with previous VHA allocation systems;

- the economic incentives created by VERA, as well as the system's major advantages and drawbacks;

- the types of changes made over the past four years in response to VERA; and

- areas in which VERA could be improved

We collected copies of all relevant documentary material from interviewees, including descriptions of the facilities maintained and the programs and services offered as well as the results of internal studies or evaluations.

Upon completion of the interviews, the lead interviewer drafted a site report and requested comments from the other staff members included in the interview. Our analysis of the information generated through the interviews focused on synthesizing the interview results and extracting a set of themes and lessons learned regarding the impact of VERA. We then used these themes and lessons, together with the data gleaned from our document and literature reviews, to address the project's three major research issues. The products of this effort are detailed in the next three chapters.

Chapter Three

THE IMPACT OF SELECTED PATIENT AND VISN CHARACTERISTICS ON CARE UNDER VERA

Recently, Congress has questioned whether the VERA system may lead to a distribution of funds that does not cover the special needs of some veterans adequately. RAND was asked to respond to several questions that address this concern from a variety of perspectives. Specifically, we were asked to analyze the impact of the allocation of funds under the VERA methodology on the following:

- VISNs and subregions with older-than-average medical facilities and infrastructures, including facilities designated as historic landmarks;

- VISNs with populations of enrolled veterans who are older or more disabled than the average population of enrolled veterans;

- VISNs undergoing major consolidation with significant attendant costs; and

- VISNs in rural and urban subregions with backlog and waiting periods for appointments.

Since these considerations are not necessarily related, we have chosen to analyze each separately. The final section of this chapter summarizes the main findings and highlights the common themes and important relationships across the four objectives.

THE MAINTENANCE OF OLDER-THAN-AVERAGE MEDICAL FACILITIES AND INFRASTRUCTURES

The VHA operates more than 47,000 buildings across its many health care delivery locations (GAO, 1999). Many of these delivery locations have large campuses comprising 16 or more buildings. A large share of these buildings, approximately 40 percent, are more than 50 years old, and nearly one-third

have historical significance.[1] These figures suggest that the use and maintenance of aging buildings, particularly those with historical significance, are important issues for the VIIA. In this section, we first discuss how the VERA
methodology funds the maintenance of medical facilities and whether the system makes any adjustments for age or historical significance. Next, we consider
the impact of the VERA methodology on maintenance and the impact of age
and historical significance on the costs of delivering health care. Finally, we
consider whether the VERA methodology should adjust for the age and historical significance of medical facilities.

Funding for Maintenance Under VERA

Under the VERA methodology, the maintenance of facilities is funded in two
ways. Basic recurring maintenance, such as cleaning and groundskeeping, is
considered to be a cost of operation and is not funded directly; rather it is
treated like office supplies or furniture and is funded out of the overall medical
care allocation. In contrast, nonrecurring maintenance (NRM) is funded
through a specific allocation within the VERA methodology. The allocation of
NRM dollars is based on the VISN workload (patients treated). The workload-
based allocation is then adjusted using the Boeckh Index to account for differences in the cost of construction across geographic areas.[2] In prior years, the
NRM allocation was also adjusted for the age and square footage of the facilities
within a VISN. However, the age and square footage adjustment has been
phased out over the past several years as the DVA moved toward an allocation
system based primarily on workload. As such, the VERA methodology does not
currently adjust in any way for differences in the age or historical significance of
facilities across VISNs (DVA, 2001).

The Impact of VERA on Maintenance

The allocation of funds under VERA does have an impact on the maintenance of
facilities and infrastructure within a VISN. During the visits to VISN centers and
facilities, some common themes emerged regarding the impact of VERA on
maintenance. We often observed that when operating budgets were strained,
needed maintenance was postponed and the NRM dollars were applied to

---

[1] In this case, age is defined as the number of years since the building was originally constructed.
However, the dates and extent of renovations to the original facility must also be considered when
examining the impact of the age of facilities on VISNs.

[2] The Boeckh Index is a construction cost index published by Marshall & Swift/Boeckh. The index
covers 11 building types and 115 cost elements. We describe use of the Boeckh Index in more detail
in Chapter 5 when we discuss whether VERA adjusts for weather-related differences in costs across
VISNs.

patient care. While all the VISN representatives recognized that this reallocation was relatively shortsighted, they believed it was necessary to meet the current needs of their patients. Another recurring theme of the interviews was the expense of maintaining the large campuses on which many VA facilities are located. VERA does not adjust for acreage, square footage, or number of buildings relative to workload when calculating NRM; thus VISNs with a greater-than-average number of large campuses could be at a distinct budgetary disadvantage over VISNs with fewer-than-average large campuses.

Many of the other issues that arise from VERA's handling of maintenance and renovation are attributable to the fact that the VHA receives maintenance and renovation funds through two different appropriations. The medical care appropriation, allocated by VERA, contains money for NRM, while the construction appropriation funds both minor (under $4 million) and major (over $4 million) construction projects. The budget approval process for minor construction funds is less rigorous than for major construction and is left to the VISN. Thus, VISNs have an incentive to invest in a number of small improvements over the course of several years rather than seek funds for a major renovation to be done at one time. Representatives of many VISNs reported having a committee of VISN engineers that annually evaluates maintenance and construction needs across the VISN. Projects are then funded according to the level of priority set by the committee.

The funding of capital assets from two different appropriations also can provide perverse incentives. Sound capital asset planning requires consideration of the relative costs and benefits of alternative renovation and construction projects. The GAO reports that in some cases, the dual funding structure led the VHA to choose capital projects that were more costly than their alternatives (GAO, 1999). As a general example, funding for leases comes from the medical care appropriation whereas funding for the construction of a new facility comes from the major construction appropriation. This distinction creates special problems for VISNs that are experiencing rapid growth in workload and are faced with an inadequate physical infrastructure to support the growth. These VISNs often lease patient care space at a much higher cost than if the VA owned the space, because they can't get approval/funds for a major construction. When funding from only one of the two appropriations is available, the VISN may not be able to choose the lowest cost alternative. Both the GAO and the Office of the Inspector General have argued that the capital asset budgeting for the VHA should be reorganized so that the funds come from a single appropriation (GAO, 1999; Office of the Inspector General, 1998).

The Impact of Age and Historical Significance on Costs

As mentioned, the VERA methodology does not currently adjust for differences in the age or historical significance of facilities across VISNs. However, this lack of adjustment does not mean that these factors do not have an impact on the cost of delivering health care to veterans. In fact, the evidence suggests quite the contrary: The age of a facility is an important determinant of the cost of doing business. Unless recently renovated, older buildings tend to be less energy efficient than their newer counterparts. In addition, many of the old, poorly maintained buildings are in large, campus-style facilities. Such campuses are typically spread out over a large area, which can make them spatially inefficient. In addition, older facilities tend to have excess inpatient capacity. This excess capacity arises from a mismatch between the current capital infrastructure and the current trends in health care toward greater use of outpatient care. Finally, the historical significance of a facility also has an important impact on the cost at the VISN level. Thus, the age and historical significance of buildings within a VISN could have an impact on the cost of delivering health care for a number of reasons. In the discussion that follows, we provide supporting evidence from our interviews and the rather limited literature. In fact, the only literature that we found relevant to the impact of facility age on the costs of delivering health care was in the form of GAO reports.

Older Buildings Have Lower Energy Efficiency Than Newer Ones. Older buildings that have not been renovated tend to be inefficient in the use of energy. This inefficiency stems from a number of sources such as leaky windows, a lack of proper insulation, and inefficient lighting. An interview with the staff of one facility in the Northeast revealed that many of their older buildings do not have the capacity for central air-conditioning. As a result, the facility uses a large number of relatively inefficient window units to cool the buildings during the summer months. On a similar note, many of the large, campus-style facilities are heated by boilers. Boiler system heating can be inefficient in that all buildings on the campus, even those not being used, are heated. Some of these inefficiencies are more easily fixed than others. Replacing light bulbs and windows is a relatively low-cost action that can be taken to improve the energy efficiency of older facilities. However, other improvements would require significant capital investments. In such cases, the construction of new facilities may be less costly than the renovation and should be considered.

Older Facilities Tend to Be Spatially Inefficient. The campus-style facilities are typically spread out over a large area and comprise a large number of buildings. As a result, such facilities are spatially inefficient. For example, one facility that we visited pointed out that the distance from one end of the facility to the other end was approximately 1.5 miles. The location of buildings over an area this size requires more staff and vehicles for tasks such as moving supplies, delivering meals, and picking up laundry than would a more compact facility. Further, facility staff believe that the campus design makes it burdensome for patients to go from one appointment to another within the facility and does not allow for consolidation of staff and sharing of programs and services. In addition, large campuses face greater groundskeeping and maintenance costs relative to workload than smaller campuses. This disparity is especially true with regard to snow removal costs in cold weather areas and mowing and watering costs in hot weather areas. Further, some large campuses face the additional costs of maintaining their own fire-fighting units at a cost to one VISN of more than $2.6 million per year. In all of the interviews we conducted, facility directors who claimed to be struggling to maintain a large, spread-out campus expressed pride in the appearance of their campuses and a determination to find unique and cost-efficient ways to keep the grounds attractive. Some facilities reported employing veterans from the domiciliary and homeless programs to assist with groundskeeping, while another reported that they employed prisoners from a local correctional facility to mow and weed the grounds.

Older Facilities Often Contain Unusable Space. The typical mix of buildings on the old campuses often does not reflect the current health care delivery needs of the facility. Many older facilities have a large number of unused inpatient beds and space that is not easily convertible to outpatient care. As evidence, the GAO reports large differences in the VHA's inpatient bed capacity compared with inpatient bed use (GAO, 1999). In 1998, inpatient bed use was approximately 55 percent of capacity. Inefficient ambulatory care space reduces the number of patients a provider can see in a clinic, thus hindering the ability to increase workload and to provide timely specialty care. The reduction in demand for inpatient beds is not unique to the VHA. On the contrary, the move toward greater use of outpatient care has been seen in community hospitals as well. In response to the trends in health care delivery, the VHA has encouraged the formation of Community-Based Outpatient Clinics (CBOCs) throughout a VISN's geographic area. At the same time, VISNs have been actively reducing the number of inpatient beds. For example, an interview of the staff of one facility revealed that the facility had reduced inpatient beds by approximately 90 percent between 1995 and 2000. One consequence of this trend is that facilities have closed inpatient wards. In some cases, particularly on the larger campuses, entire buildings have been left vacant. According to the GAO (1999), nearly 4 percent of VHA's buildings are currently vacant, with an additional 16 percent occupied by tenants. Some of the excess space within the system is leased out. However, according to one of our interviewees, much of the space is occupied by government agencies that pay no rent or pay at the minimal rate of $5.00 per square foot. The GAO argues that the VHA could reduce asset costs and provide better service to its constituency if it "reduced the level of resources spent on underused and inefficient buildings" (GAO, 1999, p. 4).

Maintenance of Historical Buildings Incurs Special Expenses. Nearly one-third of VHA buildings have historical significance (GAO, 1999). The significance of a particular site is based on a number of factors including the age, architectural style, and history of the building. Once a building has been determined to meet the criteria for listing on the National Register of Historic Places, the VHA must comply with specific procedures for maintenance, renovation, and disposal of that building. Compliance with such regulations can increase the maintenance and renovation costs of the facility significantly. For example, one facility director noted that when they wanted to replace old windows, the price difference between standard single-pane windows and the multipaned windows that the historic preservation committee suggested was approximately $300 per window. In addition to the extra replacement cost, these multipaned windows take longer to wash and thus are more costly to maintain. In such cases, the facility must face the difficult choice between incurring high costs and postponing needed maintenance. In the long run, postponing needed preventive maintenance may lead to higher costs. Consequently, medical centers with historically significant buildings face increased costs and other barriers when they wish to renovate or close facilities that no longer fulfill their health care delivery needs. On the one hand, the VERA system provides incentives to become efficient and reduce the costs of health care delivery. On the other hand, facilities with historical buildings have a limited ability to control the costs of maintenance and renovation and thus may not be able to reduce costs as much as other facilities that do not face the constraints associated with historically significant buildings.

Should VERA Adjust for Age and Historical Significance? Given the evidence provided above, it appears that the age, physical condition, and historical significance of the buildings within a VISN do have an impact on the cost of delivering health care. However, that impact does not necessarily justify modifying the VERA methodology to adjust for age, condition, and historical significance in its allocation of funds. An adjustment would be warranted only if age, condition, and historical significance have a differential impact across VISNs and are outside the control of the VISN management. A building's historical significance clearly is not under the control of the VISN. However, whether the VISN has control over the age or physical condition of its facilities is not as clear. In the private sector, if a building is inefficient, strong incentives exist to renovate that building or move to a new facility; yet within the structure of the VHA, even if the same incentives are present, the barriers to change are much more significant. The VERA methodology provides incentives to reduce costs, but VISNs do not always have the power to make the key capital and infrastructure decisions that would help them become more efficient. Consequently, we argue that since facility age is largely outside the control of VISN management, an adjustment to the VERA methodology would be warranted only if the impact of age, physical condition, and historical significance differs across VISNs. The existence of such a difference is an empirical question that can best be answered within the broader context of a comprehensive analysis of facility costs. We outline the plan for such an analysis in Chapter 6 of this report.

POPULATIONS OF ENROLLED VETERANS WHO ARE OLDER AND MORE DISABLED

The average age of patients and their level of disability are two indicators of the case mix, or level of disease burden, that a health care provider faces. In a system that allocates health care resources, differences in case mix among providers are an important concern. In this section we address the issue of case mix within the context of the VERA methodology. We begin with a general discussion of why resource allocation systems often adjust for case mix. We then turn to a description of how VERA adjusts for case mix and the effects of this adjustment on health care delivery in the VA system. We end with a discussion of potential refinements to the current method of adjusting for differences in case mix across VISNs.

The Case for Case-Mix Adjustments

Cost containment and equity in access are typically the two main concerns within a system that allocates health care resources. Across various systems, the nature of these concerns and their relative importance vary. However, the effort to balance these concerns has consistently led to some form of capitated health care financing system (Rice and Smith, 2000). The simplest form of a capitated system provides a set payment for each individual for whom the health care system has responsibility. However, expected health care expenditures vary substantially across people, depending on personal characteristics such as age and health status. Consequently, many health care systems have tried to improve upon the purely capitated system through the process of risk adjustment. Risk adjustment uses an individual's personal characteristics to estimate his or her expected health care costs relative to all other members of the health care system.

Risk adjustment can take many forms. The most basic risk adjustment processes may classify patients according to characteristics such as age or sex. Other, more refined risk adjustment processes also consider an individual's health care status. However, the type of adjustment chosen often reflects the type and reliability of the data that are available. Further, the literature provides no consensus regarding what factors should be included in the risk adjustment (Madden et al., 2000), thus contributing to the wide range of processes used.

Although capitation systems that incorporate risk adjustment are able to improve predictions of an individual's health care expenditures, a component of costs will always be unpredictable (Rice and Smith, 2001). Thus, the health care system incurs some risk in that the payment received for an individual will not necessarily match the required expenditures. Because the level of risk incurred by the system reflects in part the accuracy of the capitation payment, risk adjustment is expected to reduce, but not eliminate, the risk that a health care system faces.

How VERA Adjusts for Differences in Case Mix Across VISNs

The VERA methodology is a simple capitated system with risk adjustment. The system accounts for differences in age and level of disability through the classification of patients into three payment categories. These payment categories were designed to balance the varying health care needs of veterans with the need for an equitable and understandable funding allocation system. As described in the introduction, the three categories reflect the three general types of patients that the VA treats: Basic Non-Vested, Basic Vested, and Complex.

Since patient age is correlated with health care needs, categorizing patients into the three classifications implicitly accounts for age differences across VISNs to some extent. In addition, the VERA methodology directly accounts for age differences across VISNs in the forecast of the Complex Care workload. Complex Care use rates are computed for eight distinct age groups for each VISN in each historical fiscal year. These age-specific use rates and current population data are then used to forecast the Complex Care workload for the current fiscal year (Allocation Resource Center, 2000). Consequently, the forecasted workload reflects expected changes in the age distribution of veterans within a VISN over time.

As noted in the introduction, the VERA system allocates funding to the 22 networks, and facility allocations are determined at the VISN level. Although the methodologies used to allocate funding to facilities differ widely across VISNs, many incorporate some type of case-mix adjustment. Adjustments for case mix are particularly important in facility allocations, since facility types vary relatively widely across a VISN (for example, some are tertiary care centers, some are outpatient clinics, others are nursing homes).

The Effects of the Current Case-Mix Adjustment on the Delivery of Health Care

The VERA case-mix adjustment was designed with the VA's stated objective of providing a simple and easily understandable allocation process. The move toward a simple allocation system was motivated by problems that arose out of the previous allocation method, Resource Planning and Management (RPM), a highly complex patient-based resource allocation system. This complexity made the budget process onerous and difficult to understand. VERA was designed in response to concerns regarding the complexity of the RPM process. The VERA model's classification of patients into only three cost groups keeps the allocation system simple and makes it easy for VISN directors to predict the size of future allocations, thus allowing for better planning.

VERA May Not Adequately Adjust for Case-Mix Differences Across VISNs. While the goal of simplicity is important, it must be balanced with the goal of equity. The interviews revealed a common perception that the current case-mix adjustment does not adequately account for differences in the health status of patients across VISNs. This perception is especially strong among VISNs with a large number of tertiary care facilities. Patients are referred from other VA medical Centers (VAMCs) and VISNs to these high-tech facilities for what is often costly specialty care such as neurosurgery. Although these patients fall into the Basic Vested Care price category, the cost of providing their care far exceeds the allocation. Since tertiary care facilities provide a larger volume of costly inpatient care and must maintain the staffing levels and equipment necessary to provide high-tech care, VISNs with a higher-than-average number of these facilities may be at a distinct disadvantage with regard to VERA. Furthermore, for a patient who receives care in multiple networks, the capitated payment for that veteran is split among the VISNs that provided care. The distribution of the payment is based on each VISN's share of the total Basic Care costs for the patient during the specified three-year time frame (Allocation Resource Center, 2000). As such, VISNs will not receive the full capitated payment for every patient they treat.

The perception that the current case-mix adjustment does not account adequately for case-mix differences across VISNs is fueled by studies showing relatively wide differences in case-mix measures. For example, in a recent report on the health status and outcomes of veterans, survey results indicated that both physical and mental component scores varied by more than 50 percent of a standard deviation across the 22 networks (Center for Health Care Quality, Outcomes and Economic Research, 2000). Similarly, risk adjustment scores based on Diagnostic Cost Groups (DCGs)[3] show significant differences in case mix (Management Sciences Group, 2001). However, these studies also highlight the difficulties in accurately adjusting for case mix. The two different methodologies used lead to very different rankings of the VISNs in terms of

---

[3] The Diagnostic Cost Group risk adjustment process categorizes patients based on diagnosis, age, and gender.

disease burden. As a result, the distribution of funding across VISNs would be quite different under each method. Consequently, while most people that we spoke with would agree that the current case-mix adjustment should be refined, no general consensus emerged on exactly how it should be refined.

If the case-mix adjustment does not adequately account for differences in the average health status of veterans across VISNs, the system may contribute to inequities in access to care across networks. A VISN with a particularly difficult case mix may not be funded adequately to provide the care their patients need. One consequence of underfunding these VISNs is that they are likely to have longer backlogs and waiting periods for health care services than networks with healthier patients.

VERA's Structure Provides Incentives for Gaming the System. Whenever a capitated system of allocating resources is developed, the possibility of gaming the system must be considered. The structure of the payment to a VISN, or more generally a health plan, provides incentives that can affect the way the system is used and thus the ability of the methodology to allocate resources equitably. In general, the potential for gaming in a risk adjustment process is reduced by basing the adjustment on factors that are outside the control of the health plan. These factors often include the demographic characteristics of the patient as well as the patient's health status. However, under the VERA methodology, the utilization of VA services is used in some cases to classify patients into the Basic Care or Complex Care category. This factor creates an incentive to alter treatment in such a way as to shift a patient from the Basic Care to the Complex Care class. This incentive is magnified by the large difference in price per patient between the two classifications. The physicians interviewed for the study acknowledged this incentive and felt torn between their desire to provide the appropriate level of care and their facility's (and the VISN's) need for additional resources. The physicians also believed that this concern applied only to patients who were on the borderline between the two categories. For example, in some cases, the difference between a Basic Care and a Complex Care patient is the number of days the person stays in the hospital. If the dividing line is set at 30 days, then the physicians reported feeling tempted to keep patients an additional day or two in order to move them into the Complex Care category even if the patients were ready to be released after 28 or 29 days. While all physicians interviewed agreed that this temptation was present, none of the interviewees admitted to gaming the system in this way. In fact, many of the direct care providers we interviewed admitted to remaining intentionally unaware of the specific criteria used to determine whether a patient fell into the Basic Vested or Complex category; they did so in order to rely solely on their clinical judgment when making patient care decisions.

Under VERA, Patients Whose Care Is Well Within or Far Exceeds Their Allocation Are Clearly Identifiable. Under the current case-mix adjustment, patients whose care costs far exceed their allocation as well as those whose care costs are far less than the allotted amount may be identifiable. Some patients' health care costs are well below the price received by the VISN. For example, a veteran who comes to the VA only for a yearly exam will cost the VISN far less than the $3,126 the VISN will receive for that veteran's care. In contrast, other patients are expected to incur health care costs that are much higher than the payment the VISN will receive. An example of the latter in the Basic Care category would be an individual who is being treated for heart disease and requires coronary artery bypass surgery. On the Complex Care side, patients with a traumatic brain injury and patients who are ventilator dependent are examples of patients whose yearly costs will typically exceed the $42,765 payment that the VISN receives. In fact, one facility reported having ventilator-dependent patients whose annual costs were as high as $300,000.

The ability to identify groups of patients who will exceed or use only a small proportion of their capitated payment creates the incentive to try to attract some groups and avoid treating others. This incentive can create a problem at the individual level if veterans who are expected to need costly care are denied access to services. However, our interviews of staff at VISNs and facilities found no evidence that high-cost patients were being refused services or passed off to other facilities. In fact, we consistently found that both care providers and administrators expressed a strong commitment to veterans who require lifelong care for chronic conditions.

However, one main concern emerged in our visits with the VHA staff regarding the ability to clearly identify those patients who will or will not exceed their allotted care under the VERA system. Many staff felt a tension between the VA's mission to treat veterans in the special emphasis programs and the economic incentive to reduce costs. Many of the Complex Care categories that are expected to cost more than the allocated payment are special emphasis programs. As such, the VERA system does not provide a financial incentive to make these services available. However, the VISNs and facilities are dedicated to providing the special emphasis programs because they believe the programs are part of their mission. Consequently, they feel that they provide a great deal of care for which they are not adequately funded.

How Could the VERA Case-Mix Adjustment Be Refined?

Developing an improved case-mix methodology is an empirical issue. Before doing such an analysis, we should first think more broadly about what characteristics a new case-mix adjustment should have. First, the adjustment should not be based on utilization patterns. Rather, factors such as age, gender, and health status that are outside the control of the health care provider should be used. In this way, the incentive to manipulate utilization to influence financial allocations is minimized. Further, a new case-mix adjustment should improve the prediction of expected costs. An allocation system that accounts more accurately for the wide variation in health care expenditures across patients will be better able to match resources with needs. However, it is important to keep the goal of simplicity in mind in the development of a new case-mix adjustment. A tradeoff exists between simplicity and the accuracy of expected cost predictions, and a balance between these two desires is important.

Work groups of VISN and facility administrators are continually trying to improve the VERA system. Refining the case-mix adjustment has been one of the main issues discussed in the Patient Classification Workgroup. Further, VA researchers are conducting ongoing studies on potential changes to the existing case-mix adjustment. Currently, an adjustment based on DCGs is under consideration. The DCG process of risk adjustment is based on a patient's diagnosis, gender, and age, which meets the first criterion for improvement outlined above. Further, the accuracy of predicted expenditures under a DCG risk adjustment is an empirical question and is currently being studied by the VA's VERA Patient Classification Workgroup through the assistance of the Houston Center for Quality of Care and Utilization Studies and the Management Sciences Group (Management Sciences Group, 2000). The primary disadvantage of the DCG model that has been identified thus far is that it does not account for mental health and long-term care costs. As such, further adjustments to the DCG model are being considered.

MAJOR CONSOLIDATION OF FACILITIES AND SERVICES

As a system based on capitated payments, the VERA methodology provides strong incentives for VISNs to reduce treatment costs. Consolidation of services within a VISN is just one of the many avenues through which cost containment may be achieved. If consolidation does lead to lower costs, the question remains as to whether such cost reductions reflect greater efficiency. Efficiency gains are achieved only if the same level and quality of care are provided at a lower cost. In this section, we summarize findings from the literature and our interviews that suggest that consolidation can lead to cost savings and efficiency gains. However, we find that the barriers to consolidation of services can prevent VISNs from taking actions that could potentially reduce their costs and improve the quality of services being provided within their network.

The Effects of Consolidation

Much of the consolidation that has occurred since the implementation of the VERA methodology has been motivated by two key goals. The first goal is to reduce the duplication of services within a network. This goal assumes that consolidating clinical services by location leads to gains in efficiency through economies of scale. The second major motivation for consolidation is to shift the health care delivery infrastructure within a network to match the current delivery needs. In most cases, this type of consolidation is driven by a need to reduce the number of inpatient beds and increase outpatient services.

Reducing Duplicative Services Should Reduce Costs. In the private sector, hospital mergers and the consolidation of particular clinical services to one location within a hospital system (e.g., the treatment of all orthopedic surgery patients at one hospital) are often cited as a potential source of economic efficiencies. However, the health economics literature is not in agreement on this point. While the literature provides no consensus on overall hospital economies of scale, studies of the consolidation of more specialized hospital services have found gains in efficiency (Lynk, 1995; Vita et al., 1991; Vita, 1990; Granneman, Brown, and Pauly, 1986; Schwartz and Joskow, 1980). One source of the gains in efficiency attributed to the consolidation of specialized services is a reduction in the relative variability of random patient demand: The consolidated department faces a more stable demand for staff and is thus better able to deal with peak load demand (Lynk, 1995). These types of efficiency gains will be most prominent in clinical departments where demand is urgent and cannot be spread out over time (e.g., treatment for myocardial infarctions). It has also been argued that the consolidation of specialized services can lead to greater efficiency through improvements in the quality of care received (Luft et al., 1990). Quality improvements are generally thought to be achieved through specialization or more frequent practice of clinical skills (Luft et al., 1990).

The evidence supporting efficiency gains through consolidation is not limited to the literature on private-sector hospital systems. According to a 1999 GAO report on capital asset planning, 106 markets exist within the VHA system.[4] Nearly 40 percent of those markets have multiple delivery locations, with nine having four or more locations that serve the same patient base (GAO, 1999). In many cases, the same services are provided at multiple locations. The GAO suggested that the multiple location markets provided great opportunities for cost savings through asset restructuring. In such markets, the reduction of duplicative services typically involves the closure of one or more facilities. As an

---

[4] The GAO defines a market as a geographic area generally within 75 miles of an existing VHA major delivery location (GAO, 1999).

example, in 1998 the GAO studied the impact of closing one of the four delivery locations within the Chicago area. The study found that consolidating services into three locations could reduce VHA expenditures in that market by an estimated $200 million over the next ten years (GAO, 1998). Further, the GAO argues that the cost reductions achieved through consolidation would not have a negative impact on access to services and would allow VHA to provide higher quality care.

Consolidations Should Improve the Match Between Infrastructure and Health Care Delivery Needs. Over time, the health care industry has experienced a general shift away from inpatient treatment toward the provision of outpatient services. This shift is the result of many factors including increased interest in cost containment and improvements in medical technologies. As a result of this shift, many hospital systems have been left with unused inpatient capacity. The GAO reports that, in 1995, approximately 26 percent of community hospital beds were unused (GAO, 1999). As a result of this reduction in demand for inpatient services, many hospital systems have renovated existing buildings and built new facilities in an effort to address their changing health care delivery needs. The literature suggests that consolidations can achieve efficiency gains by creating a better match between health care delivery demands and the hospital system's infrastructure. As evidence, research has shown improvements in operating efficiency after mergers and consolidations (Alexander, Halpern, and Lee, 1996; Levitz and Brooke, 1985). The efficiency gains are seen through improvements in both occupancy rates (calculated as the ratio of the average daily census to the number of beds) and total expenses per adjusted admission.

The experience within the VHA system has mirrored that of the private sector. As a result, many VHA facilities have a large number of unused inpatient beds. In response to the reduction in demand for inpatient services, VHA has worked to reduce inpatient capacity and increase their focus on providing outpatient care. In particular, the VHA has promoted the formation of new CBOCs throughout the VHA service areas. At least two networks we visited have opened over 30 CBOCs since VERA's inception, and plans are in place to open still more.

Costs Associated with Consolidations

While consolidations can achieve cost savings in the long run, short-term costs are associated with such changes. These costs can be both pecuniary and nonpecuniary. The monetary costs incurred with consolidation include those resulting from the relocation of equipment and workload to new sites, the renovation of existing space, and the relocation of staff. Consolidations may also affect the breadth of services provided by a facility, which may result in an increase in costs over the long term. In their report on the consolidation of services in the Chicago area, the GAO estimated that it would cost between $50,000 and $100,000 to modify an inpatient ward to create additional outpatient treatment work space, although the report did not specify how many wards would need to be renovated (GAO, 1998). However, renovation of existing space is not the VHA's only alternative. Establishing new CBOCs can help to accommodate outpatient treatment that is displaced by consolidation efforts. CBOCs tend to be an efficient method of delivering health care. The GAO estimates that the average cost of establishing a new outpatient clinic is approximately $120,000 (GAO, 1998). Furthermore, these start-up costs are expected to be recovered in the long run through the CBOC's ability to meet veterans' health care needs at a lower cost (GAO, 1998). However, some VISNs reported difficulty covering CBOC activation costs from already strained budgets.

While the pecuniary costs of consolidation are relatively straightforward, the non-pecuniary costs are more subtle. Within the VHA system, consolidation proposals are considered within the framework of the VHA's mission to provide equitable access to high-quality health care for all veterans. Thus, any proposal to consolidate services must show that such changes will not reduce access to care or compromise the VHA's other health-related missions. Even if a proposed consolidation meets these criteria, it may have an impact on patient satisfaction. Although the veterans in the area where the consolidation takes place have access to all the same services, they may have to travel further or to new locations to obtain care. As a result, they may believe their access has been reduced. However, in the long term, as the VHA obtains the cost savings and is able to provide better services, patient satisfaction will likely improve. Staff morale and satisfaction may be similarly influenced by consolidations.

Barriers to Consolidation

The evidence indicates that mergers and consolidations can lead to gains in efficiency. As such, under the VERA methodology, a strong incentive exists to consolidate services in an effort to minimize costs and improve efficiency. While consolidation is generally a viable option in the private sector, VISNs may not always have the ability to make these cost-saving decisions. First, funding for consolidation efforts may not be available. In addition, VHA has a diverse group of stakeholders that includes labor unions, veterans' organizations, members of Congress, affiliated universities, and local community leaders. Consequently, any proposed changes are highly scrutinized by many parties with divergent interests. The interviews provided ample evidence that VISNs would like to close down inefficient facilities and consolidate services but believed that the external pressures against such projects are too great. At all of the large, campus-style facilities that we visited, staff voiced frustration regarding the barriers they face in downsizing the physical plant. Many of those barriers are diverse and unique to the geographic location, but similarities emerged. For example, opposition from local community leaders and veterans' groups often focused on their belief that elimination of physical structures represents elimination of services. Staff at other VISNs reported facing strong opposition from veterans' groups to consolidating special-emphasis programs such as spinal cord injury services, even though such a consolidation has the potential to improve care and reduce costs.

The GAO report on the consolidation of services in Chicago highlights the types of resistance that consolidation efforts are likely to face.[5] Much of the opposition to the proposed consolidation of services came from the medical schools affiliated with the affected hospitals. This opposition reflects the fact that the reorganization of the services provided by VHA in the Chicago market would require changes in the relationships among the affiliated medical schools (GAO, 1998). Interviews with staff at many networks with strong medical school affiliations revealed resistance on the part of the medical schools to move from an inpatient specialty model of graduate medical education to an outpatient primary care model. Thus, closing inpatient facilities and consolidating services creates tension between the VHA and their medical school affiliates.

As a result of the barriers to consolidation, many VISNs are in a difficult situation. The allocation methodology rewards cost efficiency and thus encourages VISNs to take actions to reduce costs. However, the VISNs often lack the ability to take these actions.

BACKLOGS AND WAITING PERIODS FOR APPOINTMENTS IN RURAL AND URBAN SETTINGS

The legislative language and subsequent scope of work developed by the VHA that outlined this work focused on two specific issues related to access: backlogs and waiting periods for appointments. In our analysis, we have chosen to broaden the scope to consider access issues more generally. This decision was driven in part by our review of the literature. Very little previous work speaks directly to waiting times and backlogs. However, the literature on the more general concept of access is much more developed. The VERA methodology for allocating funds has conflicting impacts on access, and these effects cut across both rural and urban settings. Under VERA, each VISN has an incentive to increase workload. This incentive derives from the fact that the allocation to a

---

[5] It should be noted that the VA did not concur with the GAO's recommendation to consolidate services by closing one of the four hospitals in the Chicago market. The VA argued that a more detailed study of all the potential options is needed.

VISN is determined in large part by the number of patients treated. As such, an increase in workload is expected to increase future allocations. However, it is important to note that the incentive is to increase the workload of relatively healthy patients for whom the VERA price will likely exceed health care expenditures. In response to the incentive to grow, some VISNs have undertaken marketing campaigns in an effort to attract new veterans, while others have focused on opening new CBOCs. While a number of factors have led to the proliferation of CBOCs, one of the main benefits of this growth for VISNs has been the increase in the number of patients treated. The incentive to grow has clear benefits for access. VISNs are providing new health care delivery locations that typically reduce the distance veterans have to travel to receive VA health care.

However, the negative impact of growth on access to care is less obvious. Under the VERA methodology, the calculation of the Basic Care Workload may not reflect recent growth in the number of patients treated. Thus, the current fiscal year allocation may not be adequate. As a result, VISNs may not have the funds necessary to provide services to the growing number of patients without increasing backlogs and waiting periods. Ultimately, the opposing effects of VERA on access make the net effect an empirical question.

In the following discussion, we analyze the impact of VERA on access to care, incorporating the findings from our interviews and the review of the literature. We first provide more detail on the beneficial impacts of VERA on access to care and then turn to the detrimental effects on access. While the major impacts of VERA on access to care cut across both urban and rural settings, the final section highlights differences in the cost of providing health care in urban and rural networks.

Beneficial Impacts of VERA on Access

Through the incentive to grow, the VERA methodology has a beneficial impact on access to care. Since the implementation of VERA in 1997, many new CBOCs have been established, and the number of veterans served has increased substantially. The increase in utilization associated with the CBOCs is driven in large part by the placement of the clinics. VISNs have typically focused on opening CBOCs in areas that had been previously underserved. Evidence from the health care literature supports this practice: Several studies have shown that people are more likely to obtain basic health care if the provider is located within his or her daily "activity space" (Nemet and Bailey, 2000; Cromley and Shannon, 1986). Although these studies are relatively small-scale and focus primarily on one geographic area, the results appear applicable to the general population. Reducing the distance that a veteran has to travel to receive care reduces in turn the overall cost of care to the individual (Bosanac, Parkinson, and Hall, 1976; Bronstein and Morrissey, 1990). Thus, providing delivery locations that are closer to the veteran's home improves the likelihood that he or she will obtain care through the VA system. It should be noted that it is particularly difficult to open CBOCs in very rural areas, as the number of veterans may be insufficient to support the clinic. As such, the improvement in access generated through the growth in CBOCs may not be distributed evenly across VISNs.

The average distance veterans must travel to receive care varies widely across VISNs. A recent study of rural health care in the VHA system reported that straight-line distances range from an average of 10 miles in VISN 3 to 84 miles in VISN 20 (AMA Systems, Inc., March 2000).[6] As a result, the impact of establishing new CBOCs on access to care is likely to vary across VISNs as well.

The proliferation of CBOCs is only one way in which VISNs have tried to increase the number of patients served. Many of the VISN representatives interviewed for the study reported actively recruiting new patients through a variety of venues. Some of the recruitment techniques used included direct-mail campaigns to local veterans, media campaigns, activities at local veterans' service organizations, and booths at local health fairs. The goal of these activities is to increase awareness about the health care services and benefits that are available for veterans in their community. However, in some VISNs in the southern and western regions, the veteran population is growing rapidly, and recruitment has been unnecessary. In one VISN, staff reported that the workload was "crushing" and that all CBOC appointments are filled within a day or two of opening.

Detrimental Impacts of VERA on Access

While the incentive under the VERA methodology to increase workload has beneficial impacts on access to care, the method used to predict workload has had an opposing effect. Although different methodologies are used to forecast workload for Basic and Complex Care patients, neither fully reflects recent growth in the number of patients served.

Workload forecasts for Basic Care patients are based on the number of eligible veterans who have used VA services during three prior years. The potential difficulty stems from the three years that are included in the workload estimate and the simplicity of the workload forecast methodology: Data from FY 1997,

---

[6] AMA Systems, Inc. noted that the straight-line distances reported may not accurately reflect travel distances, particularly in more rural VISNs. Geographic barriers such as rivers and mountain ranges may increase the distance that veterans must travel to obtain VA health care services. In more urban areas, straight-line travel distances may not reflect the actual travel time because of traffic congestion.

1998, and 1999 were used to predict the Basic Care workload for FY 2001 (DVA, 2001). If substantial growth in workload is occurring over time, relying on utilization data from previous years to predict workload may be problematic, because the older data from prior years do not reflect the current number of patients being served. Thus, VISNs that have grown during the data lag may not receive enough resources to serve the current workload, a common theme in all our interviews. Some VISNs reported that this problem has led to increases in waiting times and backlogs, because they have been unable to hire the staff needed or acquire the space necessary to serve the growing number of patients. These findings suggest that it could be beneficial to employ a sophisticated method of predicting future Basic Care workload. A forecasting methodology that accounted for growth over time would likely improve the match between predicted and actual workload.

One of the most common concerns that we encountered during our interviews was that two-year-old data are used to calculate the VISNs' funding allocation. However, it is important to note that this widely held perception is not technically correct. The VERA system uses the most recent complete years of utilization data that are available to calculate workload. This disconnect between what VERA does and how it is perceived stems from the fact that VISN and facility representatives tend to view the allocations as a reimbursement for past treatment rather than a prospective budget based on an estimate of workload for the coming year.

The definition of "eligible veterans" in the Basic Care workload has also raised some concern across the VISNs. For the purposes of the Basic Care workload calculation, eligible veterans are defined as Category A veterans—those with service-connected disabilities and/or financial need as determined by the VHA "means" test. These are the veterans who have been traditionally served by the VHA. Category A Veterans are further classified into Priority Groups 1 through 6 and 7a (see Eligibility Group description in Appendix D). All other Priority 7 Category C veterans do not have service-connected disabilities or financial need according to the "means" test. Veterans in Priority Group 7c are not included in the Basic Care workload calculation; however, treatment for these veterans is expected to be covered by the VISNs' Basic Care allocation.[7] This situation creates a problem, because the activities that VISNs undertake to increase workload (opening CBOCs and marketing campaigns) attract all types of veterans, not just Category A veterans. As a result, the growth in the number of patients being served is larger than the growth in workload as defined by VERA. This disparity becomes particularly problematic if the new veterans being

---

[7] Third-party billing and copayments are also collected to pay for the care that Priority 7 veterans receive.

brought into the system are primarily Priority 7c veterans. Access to care may be affected negatively if the Basic Care allocation to the VISN does not reflect the total number of patients served. The inclusion of Priority 7c veterans in the Basic Care workload calculation is currently under consideration by the VA, but a decision was made not to include this workload in the FY 2002 VERA methodology. The potential funding of Priority 7c veterans through the VERA Basic Care component raises concern. VISNs experiencing significant growth in all priority groups worry that funds that could be used to treat more Priority 1 through 6 veterans (Category A) in high-volume areas will be diverted to care for veterans in the Priority 7c category.

The age of the data used to predict the Complex Care workload was also cited by VISNs as a problem. The Complex Care workload prediction is a forecasted trend based on five years of data on the number of veterans who used Complex Care services. For FY 2001, FY 1995 through FY 1999 data were used to forecast the Complex Care workload (DVA, 2001). However, the use of older data is likely to be less problematic for the Complex Care workload prediction than for Basic Care because of the use of the forecasting trend methodology. Problems would arise only if the current growth rate in the Complex Care workload is significantly different from the trend during the five years of data used.

Although the incentive under VERA to increase workload has some beneficial impacts on access to care, the long-term effects of such growth may have the opposite effect. Under VERA, the allocation of funds to VISNs is based primarily on workload. As a result, each individual VISN has an incentive to increase the number of patients that it serves. As described in the introduction, the system as a whole can be seen as a zero-sum game. A set amount of money is allocated to the VISNs. The amount that VISNs receive per patient is the ratio of the total allocation to national workload. As a result, when the allocation is set and the workload increases, the price per patient falls. Thus, a VISN's allocation may fall even though its workload has increased. Further, a VISN's share of the total allocation will decrease under the VERA system if it does not grow as quickly as other VISNs. In the long run, access problems may occur if the allocation from Congress for VA health care does not keep pace with the growth in workload. In such a case, the price per patient would fall, and VISNs would be required to provide care to more patients with fewer dollars per patient. This observation suggests that the incentive to increase workload would be dampened if VISNs could collude and agree to minimize workload so that the capitated payment per patient would increase.

Differential Costs of Health Care Delivery in Urban and Rural Settings

The health services literature indicates that potential differences exist between the cost of providing health care in urban settings and that in rural settings. The differences across rural and urban settings derive mainly from differences in staffing and practice patterns. Findings from both the literature on private-sector health care and our interviews indicate that rural areas typically have fewer specialists than do urban areas, because rural areas have more difficulty recruiting and retaining specialists (Jones and Brand, 1995; Council on Graduate Medical Education, 1998). For a number of reasons, new doctors are less likely to establish practices in rural areas. Rural areas provide less opportunity for professional development and continuing education than do urban areas. In addition, rural areas may not provide enough patients for a specialist to maintain a full practice. As a result, VHA facilities in rural areas often do not have a large number of specialists on staff and must refer patients out for specialty treatment. The length of time a patient must wait for a specialty care appointment is limited by contracts and what the community and other regional VA facilities can provide. In one facility we visited, staff reported waits of over 300 days for a VA specialty appointment in urology and audiology. Staff at another rural facility we visited reported that patients who need elective surgical procedures in the associated urban VAMC must wait over 500 days for the surgery to be performed.

Within the VA system, facilities that refer patients into specialty treatment have two basic options. They can pay on a fee-for-service basis for the patient to receive specialty care in the community if such care is available, or they can send the patient to a VA specialist in a more urban delivery location. The rural facilities included in our interviews reported that treatment in the local community often required an extensive wait for an appointment and was very expensive because of low competition for specialist services. Similarly, staff at these facilities reported that when referring a patient to another VA site, waiting times for appointments can be long, and these visits can be expensive as well, since such referral often requires transportation and lodging costs for staff, beneficiaries, and accompanying family members. Under VERA, no mechanism exists to help cover the transportation costs that rural VISNs face. In many cases, though, veterans' groups have developed programs to help fill this need. In a number of interviews, we heard that veterans' groups were helping to provide transportation to and from medical appointments. Similarly, one rural facility uses a bus that was donated to them to help provide transportation between the facility and the urban tertiary care center. Given the difficulties outlined above, rural facility directors argue that their location makes it costly to provide specialty care to the veterans they serve.

On the other side of the issue, urban facilities that receive referrals from their rural counterparts provide services that are likely to be relatively high cost. In addition, many urban facility directors reported difficulty recruiting specialists because the VA salary structure is not competitive. Some argued that if this situation persisted, waiting times and backlogs for specialty services could increase in the future.

Health care staffing patterns differ significantly across urban and rural settings in other ways that also may influence the cost of providing care. The descriptive results from the peer-reviewed literature indicate that nonmetropolitan areas have fewer physicians per capita than do metropolitan areas (Himes and Rutrough, 1994). In addition, rural areas typically make greater use of physician assistants and nurse practitioners. Using nationally representative data from 1994, one study found that physician assistants or nurse practitioners were present at 37 percent of rural outpatient visits compared with only 5 percent of urban outpatient visits (Anderson and Hampton, 1999). These differences in staffing patterns in the private sector are mirrored in VA staffing patterns. According to the results of a recent case-study report on rural health care in the VA, VA staff believed that in order to increase enrollment and retain existing patients, it was important for the VA to provide health care that was similar to that found in the private sector (AMA Systems, Inc., March 2000). The results of this survey suggest that an increased use of physician assistants and nurse practitioners may be acceptable at rural facilities but might not be desirable in more urban settings. As such, rural facilities could face lower staffing costs than their urban counterparts who need to have more physicians in order to remain competitive with alternative sources of care.

Should the VERA Methodology Adjust for the Rural/Urban Nature of VISNs?

Based on our review of the literature and the information collected during our site visits, we do not believe that an adjustment for the urban/rural nature of a network is warranted at this time. While the costs of providing care appear to be affected by aspects of the networks' urban or rural nature, the effects are in opposing directions. Thus, costs do not appear to be systematically different between urban and rural VISNs. However, we do believe that VISN characteristics that are associated with its rural or urban nature, such as the average travel distance to the facility, should be included in a comprehensive model of facility-level costs. The analysis plan that we outline in Chapter 6 of this report incorporates such factors.

SUMMARY OF FINDINGS

Although the topics for analysis included in this chapter are somewhat dis-parate in nature, some common themes emerge. We find that two potential adjustments to the VERA methodology warrant further study. First, evidence suggests that health care delivery costs may be affected by the age and physical condition of a VISN's capital infrastructure. Thus, we recommend a quantita-tive analysis of this issue to determine the extent of such effects at the VISN level.

Based on our findings, the second potential change to the VERA methodology that we believe should be considered is a refinement of the current case-mix adjustment. As noted previously, the VA is considering using a DCG-based case-mix methodology in the future.

Our findings suggest that it is important that any potential adjustment not be considered in isolation. Rather, adjustments should be considered in the broader context of a comprehensive health care delivery cost model. As illus-trated by Figure 1.2, many factors influence VA health care delivery. The inter-actions between such factors necessitate analyses that account for the context in which the VA operates. As evidence, results from our site visits highlight the importance of the constraints that VISNs face on their ability to minimize costs.

Chapter Four

THE COSTS OF ACADEMIC AFFILIATIONS UNDER VERA

The major health care missions of the DVA are to provide patient care and to support research and medical education. Among the goals of the VERA system are to provide adequate support for education and research activities and to improve accountability for the use of those funds. One of the tasks of the present study was to investigate issues associated with the DVA's affiliations with medical schools and their teaching hospitals. In carrying out the task, we were asked to consider three issues:

- the costs and other requirements for maintaining affiliations;

- whether VERA takes affiliations into account in allocating funds; and,

- the role of state-of-the-art equipment in maintaining affiliations, including the costs of training personnel to use the equipment.

OVERVIEW OF DVA ACADEMIC AFFILIATIONS

Currently, 118 of 140 VHA facilities have affiliations or associations with 107 medical schools that involve varying degrees of interdependence.[1] The affiliations are considered mutually beneficial to the VHA and the medical schools. The affiliations facilitate VHA physician recruitment and retention and increase access to specialist services. For the medical schools, the VAMCs provide the faculty, patients, and facilities to support educational programs. About 70 percent of VHA physicians hold faculty appointments at medical schools (Office of the Inspector General, 1997). The VHA funds 8,700 full-time equivalent (FTE) residents or about 9 percent of the residency positions in the United States (JAMA, 2000). In addition, about 18,000 medical students and 63,000 trainees in other health professions receive some or all of their training each year in VAMCs (personal communication with DVA staff, 2001).

_____

[1]Most affiliation agreements are directly between the facilities and medical schools, although the agreements in at least one network have been transferred to the VISN.

We examined the distribution of resident positions and research funding across VISNs.[2] All 22 VISNs are involved in medical education and research. However, the level of involvement varies across and within VISNs. The number of funded resident positions in FY 2001 ranges from a high of 728 in VISN 22 to a low of 230 in VISN 19. The level of research activity also differs considerably across VISNs. Three VISNs (Boston, San Francisco, and Long Beach) account for one-third of the total funded research reported for FY 1999. The differences in the distribution of education and research activities have implications for the equity of the allocation system only if the presence of residents and other trainees and/or research affects patient care costs in ways that are not recognized by VERA.

VERA is only one aspect of the changes occurring within the VHA and the private health care sector that may be affecting academic affiliations. Other important changes include the following:

- **VHA Downsizing and Realignment of Residency Programs.** Over a three-year period beginning with the 1997–98 academic year, the VHA eliminated 250 residency positions and realigned 750 positions from medical and surgical specialties to primary care.

- **Shift from Inpatient to Ambulatory Services.** The shift toward outpatient services has been accompanied by a substantial increase in training that occurs in ambulatory settings.

- **Financial Pressures on Academic Health Centers.** Medicare funding reductions and managed care competitive pressures have placed financial pressure on academic health centers. Falling hospital and faculty practice plan revenues have increased the emphasis on clinical productivity and may reduce the willingness of academic health centers to rotate residents to VHA facilities to provide physician specialty care at no charge and supplement VHA salaries.

WHAT ARE THE COSTS AND OTHER REQUIREMENTS FOR MAINTAINING ACADEMIC AFFILIATIONS?

We believe that the fundamental issue underlying our examination of the costs and other requirements for maintaining academic affiliations is whether VERA allocates existing funds equitably. To make this assessment, we believe it is important to consider the net impact of educational and research activities on

---

[2] Comparable information on medical students and other trainees is not available. However, there is a high correlation between the number of residents and the number of medical students and other health trainees (DVA Education Model Workgroup, draft issue paper, undated).

costs. Therefore, we sought information through a literature review and from our interviews on both the benefits and costs of these missions. Costs involve not only the costs directly associated with educational and research activities but the effect of teaching and research on other patient care costs as well.

Requirements for Maintaining Academic Affiliations

Formal requirements for maintaining academic affiliations are established by the accrediting bodies for the educational programs. For example, the Liaison Committee for Medical Education establishes accreditation requirements for medical schools and clinical clerkships for medical students. The Accreditation Council for Graduate Medical Education (ACGME) establishes institutional requirements for all residency programs. Both organizations require that the educational program operate under the control of its sponsoring institution (Liaison Committee on Medical Education, 1998; American Medical Association, 1999).

The ACGME requirements are intended to ensure that educational objectives are not sacrificed to the service needs of the facilities participating in an approved residency program. In addition, Residency Review Committees (RRCs) establish specialty-specific requirements, some of which have cost implications for the participating institutions. Generally, these requirements are designed to ensure the following:

- The patient population (number and type of conditions) is adequate;

- Physician supervision is sufficient;

- Resident patient load is reasonable; and,

- The resident complement (maximum and, in some cases, minimum number of positions and/or the presence of other residency programs) is appropriate.

Ten VAMCs sponsor or are the primary clinical training site for residency programs, and another 94 are major participating institutions in residency programs (JAMA, 2000). During our interviews, we found that for most specialties, the VHA's unique patient mix is not broad and representative enough for the VHA to sponsor a residency program. Thus, the affiliations are critical to continued participation in graduate medical education. Major participating institutions generally provide six months or more of training over the course of the residents' training program, and this training must be approved by the RRC. A key factor for participation is maintaining the patient load and physician staffing to meet the RRC requirements. Patient volume and services offered by individual VHA facilities have been affected by the reduction in inpatient capacity, increased emphasis on primary care, and consolidation of specialized services. We learned during our interviews that the VA facilities have needed to work with their medical schools to adjust resident rotations and participation. VA officials at one facility reported that the facility lost its surgical residents because it no longer had sufficient patient load to keep a full-time surgeon on staff to supervise residents. This loss of residents was leading in turn to additional loss in patient volume. Others reported during the interviews that they had experienced few difficulties in working with their medical schools to adjust to the changes in service capacity. While relatively more training is taking place in ambulatory settings, we were told that this training continues to occur on the main campuses of the facilities and has not shifted to the CBOCs.

Several interviewees mentioned that the recruitment process for physician specialists who will hold faculty appointments requires coordination and negotiation with the medical school to satisfy both service and educational needs. Difficulties in recruiting and retaining highly qualified physicians who are interested in academic medicine were frequently mentioned. Most often, these difficulties were attributed to limitations on physician salaries rather than funding levels. The interviewees noted that the limits make it difficult to compete with private-sector health care providers and to meet any salary expectations that the medical school might have for VHA physicians who hold joint appointments. Several suggested that recruitment might be more difficult in market areas with multiple medical schools that compete for academic physicians.

Benefits of Academic Affiliations

Our interviews revealed that the academic affiliations provide a number of benefits to VHA facilities. Frequently cited benefits included the following:

- **Physician Recruitment and Retention.** The role of academic affiliations in recruiting and retaining highly qualified physicians was the most commonly cited benefit. Interviewees consistently noted that the opportunities for a medical school appointment and for teaching and research help counter the effects of the caps on physician salaries. In addition, a few sites noted that the medical schools helped supplement VHA salaries. At one VISN, we learned that a highly qualified physician who wanted to remain in academic medicine left when the VHA facility's academic affiliation was terminated. With respect to other health professions, we found that training programs not only help attract professionals who are interested in academic medicine but also create a pool of former students who can be recruited to fill staff vacancies.

- **Enhanced Quality of Care.** Another benefit that was mentioned frequently during the interviews was the perceived impact of the academic affiliation on quality of care. The interviewees noted that teaching and research responsibilities keep faculty current in their skills and knowledge of state-of-the-art medical care.

- **Improved Access to Specialized Services.** Affiliation agreements provide access to specialists on the medical school faculty. Several interviewees commented that their affiliation gave patients access to specialist services that the VHA facility could not afford to provide through its own staff because of budget and patient workload considerations. Others noted the benefits of agreements for shared services that provide access to a broader spectrum of services and state-of-the-art equipment than the VHA facility could maintain on its own.

- **Provision of Patient Care Services by Residents.** The interviews revealed mixed opinions on the benefits of having residents provide patient care services under faculty supervision. It was generally acknowledged that residents reduce the patient workload of attending physicians and reduce hospital-based physician staffing needs. As discussed in the next section on costs of educational benefits, others noted that teaching—particularly medical students—was time-consuming. Nursing education had less impact on patient care productivity because the educational program provides its own instructors.

- **Increased Research Opportunities.** The academic affiliations attract external funding for research and provide opportunities for collaborative research efforts.

Similar benefits were also reported in the literature on health care provider–academic affiliations (Mirvis et al., 1994; Commonwealth Fund, 1999; Office of the Inspector General, 1997; National Health Policy Forum, 1998).

Costs of Maintaining Academic Affiliations

The joint production of patient care, education, and research makes it difficult to measure the costs of education and research. Some costs can be directly attributable to education and research, while others are reflected in the impact that teaching and research activities have on physician productivity and patient-care costs.

Costs Directly Associated with Teaching Activities. Costs that can be directly attributable to teaching activity include the following:

- resident and other trainee stipends: with the exception of a limited number of stipends for advanced practitioners who contribute to patient care (e.g., trainees in dentistry, psychology, and social work), the VHA pays stipends only to residents;

- physician time spent in teaching and supervising residents;

- physician, resident, and other professional staff time spent teaching and supervising medical students and other health trainees (nursing programs generally provide their own instructors when students are training in VHA facilities); and

- associated administrative and facility costs.

One issue that emerged during the interviews was that the resident supervision rules and documentation requirements for third-party billing were burdensome and time-consuming. At the same time, it was also noted that funding constraints were increasing the emphasis on patient panel size and clinical productivity. Together, these factors were cited as making it increasingly more difficult to preserve protected time for education. These pressures are similar to those being felt by non-VA teaching physicians.

We determined during the interviews that it will be difficult to establish whether teaching time has been reduced under VERA. The costs that are reported in the accounting system are based on the amounts allocated to educational activities rather than the actual costs for those activities. For example, 20 percent of a teaching physician's compensation may be supported by the education funds and would be reported as an educational cost, but because of patient care demands, the physician may not be able to set aside this amount of time for teaching. This problem limits the ability to examine empirically the actual costs directly associated with educational activities.

Several findings emerge from our review of the literature concerning costs directly attributable to residency training in civilian hospitals. These findings could have implications for the allocation of funds to support educational activity. The most important finding is that the costs directly associated with residency programs decrease as the number of residents increases (Campbell, Gillespie, and Romeis, 1991; Council on Graduate Medical Education, 2000). One reason is that meeting accreditation standards entails some fixed education costs that do not vary with the size of the residency program. Another reason is that larger programs incur lower physician supervision costs per resident (Council on Graduate Medical Education, 2000). If this finding is also applicable to VA facilities, per-resident costs might be higher in those VISNs where the number of residents at each facility is relatively low compared with VISNs where residents are concentrated in large tertiary care centers. Another potentially important finding from the literature is that ambulatory-intensive programs are more expensive than inpatient-oriented programs, because of the higher physician-to-resident ratios in ambulatory settings. In the inpatient setting, faculty can teach multiple students at different educational levels during rounds. Residents assist teaching physicians and reduce the time faculty spend providing patient care services. Teaching in the ambulatory setting is less efficient. Patients are generally available only for short periods of time, and space constraints typically preclude teaching multiple students at the same time. Again, if this finding is applicable to VA facilities, per-resident costs might be higher in those VISNs where a relatively high proportion of the training occurs in ambulatory settings.

Costs Directly Attributable to Research Activities. A number of costs are directly attributable to research activities:

- clinical investigator and other investigator salaries;

- associated administrative and research facility costs; and

- patient-care services that are furnished solely as part of the research protocol and are not reimbursed through research project funds.

FY 1999 funded research totaled $752 million, exclusive of animal research and administrative costs. This figure includes research funded through VA appropriations as well as external sources of funding. A new research support accounting system is being implemented to account for funds to support the salaries of clinical investigators, research facilities, and administrative costs. We were advised that, as is the case with educational activities, the amounts obligated and expended (for researcher salaries) are based on allocated funds for research support rather than the actual research expenses.

Effect of Teaching and Research on Patient Care Costs. In addition to generating costs that are directly associated with teaching and research activities, academic affiliations can affect other patient care costs. In the civilian sector, teaching hospitals have a more resource-intensive practice style than nonteaching hospitals, after controlling for differences in case mix. At the same time, residents, medical students, and other trainees provide some patient care services. Research activities such as clinical trials are common to teaching hospitals and may increase patient care costs in subtle ways. For example, nursing costs may be increased by the additional time and skill required to administer and monitor the effects of experimental medications. The critical issue is how, on balance, academic affiliations affect financial performance and productivity.

The studies that have been done to date on the effect of teaching and research activities on patient care costs are not directly relevant to the VERA system.

VERA is a capitated system that encompasses both inpatient and outpatient facility services as well as physician services. Most studies have focused on the effect of teaching and research activities only on hospital inpatient costs and predate the shift of services to ambulatory settings. The one study to date that investigated whether practice patterns and infrastructure affect per capita health care costs did not explore whether teaching and research activities might explain cost differences across VISNs (AMA Systems, Inc., July 2000). Also, some findings applicable to civilian teaching hospitals may not apply to VHA facilities. Civilian teaching hospitals tend to have a higher case mix and poorer population than nonteaching civilian hospitals (Goldfarb and Coffey, 1987). Since DVA patients as a group are sicker and poorer than patients treated in civilian hospitals (Wilson and Kizer, 1997), the differences in the types of patients treated in VHA facilities with major academic affiliations and those treated in other VHA facilities may not be as great.

Nevertheless, several issues addressed in the general literature may apply to an analysis of the VERA methodology. The first issue concerns the effect of teaching on facility (nonphysician) patient care costs. Studies indicate civilian hospitals with residency programs tend to have higher inpatient costs per discharge than nonteaching hospitals after controlling for other factors such as wage differences and case mix. The higher facility costs are attributable to severity of patient illness that is not measured by the case-mix system, a more resource-intensive practice style, and teaching and research activities. The costs increase as teaching intensity (for example, the ratio of residents to beds) increases (Anderson and Lave, 1986; Dalton and Norton, 2000; Dalton, Norton, and Kilpatrick, 2001; Phillips, 1992; Rogowski and Newhouse, 1992; Sheingold, 1990; Thorpe, 1988; Welch, 1987). A study by the Health Care Financing Administration that examined the teaching effect on hospital outpatient services found only a small teaching effect on hospitals with relatively high teaching intensity (Department of Health and Human Services, 1998).

A second issue examined in the literature is the impact of teaching on the provision of patient care services by teaching physicians. Faculty time spent reviewing cases with residents and medical students and documenting in the medical record reduces the amount of time available for patient care services. As previously discussed, the net impact on physician productivity is more likely to be a cost issue in ambulatory settings. In civilian outpatient settings, studies suggest that the net effect of residency training on physician productivity is site dependent and is influenced by factors such as the amount of time spent on teaching relative to patient care, patient flow, and provider efficiency. The studies support a widespread belief that over the course of a residency program, residents have no effect on net productivity in the ambulatory setting. In other words, the value of the services provided by the resident is sufficient to offset the value of physician time spent in teaching and supervising the residents. In contrast, medical students reduce the patient care productivity of the physicians and/or the residents involved in their education (Boex, 1992; Boex et al., 1998; Council on Graduate Medical Education, 2000; Lave, 1989; Philibert, 1999).

Taken together, the results of these studies underscore the need to analyze the potential effects of teaching on per capita costs. A substantial body of literature indicates that inpatient facility costs are higher in major teaching facilities than in other facilities. While this might lead to the expectation that the major teaching facilities have higher inpatient costs than other facilities, the effect is not clear when physician and resident services are also taken into account. With respect to outpatient services, the literature suggests that the largest teaching impact is on physician costs rather than on facility costs.

Studies examining the effect of academic affiliations on VHA health care costs predate VERA and have somewhat mixed findings.

- A study by Hao and Pegels (1994) supports a finding that academic affiliations increase patient care costs. A higher proportion of the VHA facilities with membership in the College of Teaching Hospitals (generally those with major academic affiliations) were inefficient (higher cost) relative to the nonmember facilities. The inefficiencies were largely attributable to higher labor costs. College of Teaching Hospitals (COTH) members used their capital assets more efficiently but had higher staffing ratios than did the non-COTH members.

- Lehner and Burgess (1995) also found that the net effect of residents is to reduce patient care efficiency slightly. However, they also concluded that measurement error (particularly for physician and resident inputs) confounds any estimation of the effect of teaching on patient care costs.

- In contrast, Campbell and colleagues (1991) found that the higher patient care costs associated with academic affiliations were offset by resident contributions to patient care. In particular, VHA facilities with larger staffs use residents more efficiently. As a result, residents in these facilities reduce patient care costs (Campbell, Gillespie, and Romies, 1991). The study found that when the teaching subsidy for higher patient care costs was eliminated under the Resource Allocation Method in FY 1989, the financial performance of teaching hospitals was no worse than that of nonteaching hospitals.

More recently, the Residency Realignment Committee (DVA, 1996) looked explicitly at the costs associated with replacing residents. The committee estimated that net replacement costs were more than two times the hourly rate paid for resident services. Taken to a logical conclusion, the analysis suggests that facilities with a high complement of residents should have lower physician staffing needs than those with no or few residents. However, the existing pattern of physician and resident staffing in VHA facilities indicates the contrary. When we compared the physician staffing ratios in the 8 VISNs with higher-than-average ratios of residents per 1,000 unique patients to the physician staffing ratio in the remaining 14 VISNs, we found that the weighted average ratio of physicians per 1,000 unique patients in the more teaching-intensive VISNs is 4.1 compared with 3.0 in the less teaching-intensive VISNs. The average ratio (weighted by number of unique Basic Vested and Complex patients in each VISN) is 2.82 residents per 1,000 unique patients. We note that these ratios have not been adjusted for research time and other factors that might reduce the amount of time for teaching and patient care. Nevertheless, they raise an issue regarding how to determine whether physician staffing levels are consistent with what is needed for efficient delivery of patient care in an academic setting. If historical funding practices encouraged inefficient staffing patterns that have continued to the present, using these staffing patterns in an analysis of the effect of teaching activities might distort the results. This issue warrants further investigation before an empirical analysis to examine the effects that teaching might have on patient care costs is undertaken.

Medicare Support for Costs Associated with Academic Affiliations

As part of our literature review, we investigated how the Medicare program supports costs associated with academic affiliations. The purpose was to see whether some policies might pertain to VHA facilities. The Medicare program makes an explicit payment for the costs directly attributable to residency training programs. The payment is based on Medicare's share of a hospital-specific historical cost per resident that is updated for inflation and the number of FTE residents training at the hospital. The payment is intended to cover Medicare's share of resident stipends and fringe benefits, teaching physician supervision of resident services, and overhead costs directly associated with the teaching activity. Hospitals file an annual cost report that states, among other things, their current costs for graduate medical education. The average per-resident cost exclusive of resident stipends and fringe benefits for cost reporting periods beginning in FY 1997 was $55,000 (Council on Graduate Medical Education, 2000). This amount does not include costs directly associated with training medical students or other health trainees. Other than a relatively small number of provider-operated nursing and allied health training programs, Medicare does not share in the costs directly associated with training medical students and other allied health trainees.

In addition to the per-resident payment for graduate medical education, Medicare makes an add-on payment to the per-discharge Diagnosis Related Group rate paid to teaching hospitals for inpatient services. The payment is based on the empirical findings that teaching has an effect on hospital inpatient costs. The payment amount is based on each hospital's ratio of residents to beds.[3] However, teaching hospitals do not receive higher payments under Medicare's prospective payment system for hospital outpatient services, because a teaching effect on outpatient facility costs was small (Department of Health and Human Services, 1998).

The Medicare Payment Advisory Commission (MedPAC) recently evaluated the Medicare payment methodologies for the higher costs of teaching hospitals. The Commission found that the Medicare distinction between the costs directly attributable to graduate medical education and the teaching effect on patient care costs is artificial. MedPAC's reasoning is that residents provide patient care services and that Medicare's per-resident payment (analogous to VERA's education support funds plus resident stipends) represents the net value of the patient care services residents provide. MedPAC suggests that to reflect the added costs of training activities on patient care appropriately, a single supplemental payment for teaching activities should be made through patient care payments (Medicare Payment Advisory Commission, 1999, 2000).

DOES VERA ACCOUNT FOR COSTS OF MAINTAINING ACADEMIC AFFILIATIONS?

Costs Funded Outside VERA

Some costs directly associated with maintaining academic affiliations are funded outside VERA:

- Resident and other health trainee stipends are funded directly from the Medical Care appropriation. The FY 2000 funding for resident and other health trainee stipends totaled $408 million.

- Research projects are funded through the DVA Research appropriation and external grants as well as the Medical Care appropriation. The Research appropriation provides support for research costs other than those for clinical investigators, research facilities, and administrative staff. These costs are funded from the Medical Care appropriation

---

[3] The current payment level exceeds the empirically justified amount. The Medicare Payment Advisory Commission recently estimated that inpatient costs increase 3.1 percent for each .10 increment in the resident-to-bed ratio (Medicare Payment Advisory Commission, 2000).

through VERA. The FY 2001 Research appropriation totaled $351 million. Additional funding for research projects is provided through extramural grants, the General Post Fund, and nonprofit Medical Center Research Corporations.

Support Costs Funded Through VERA

Education and research support costs are funded explicitly from Medical Care appropriations as part of the VERA system. These funds are intended to cover costs that directly support teaching and research activities.

Education Support ($357 million in FY 2001). Education support funds are allocated to VISNs based on the number of funded residency positions. However, the funds are intended to cover costs directly associated with training medical students and other health trainees as well as residents. A DVA study conducted when VERA was first implemented found a high correlation between number of residents and education support costs (.90) and the number of medical students and other health trainees (.73). Since resident positions are funded and other trainees typically are not, the study concluded that the resident count is a more reliable and easier-to-track measure of educational activity. The number of non-compensated trainees and the amount of time they spend at the VHA facility is determined at the local level and could be subject to "gaming" if the counts were used to allocate education support funds (DVA Education Model Workgroup, undated).

The interviews demonstrated general agreement with the methodology used to allocate education support costs. However, we did encounter some misunderstanding that the VHA "doesn't pay for" the costs associated with training medical students and other trainees, since these trainees are not included in the allocation formula. The education support costs for these trainees were included in the historical costs used to establish the original level of education support funding under VERA. Nevertheless, a potential issue arises regarding the erosion of the funding levels over time. The FY 1997 allocation was based on the amount reported in FY 1995 for education support, inflated 5.88 percent for the two-year increase in the total DVA budget. The resulting amount equated to an education support allocation of $43,274 per resident in FY 1997. Based on the support to education estimated in the President's FY 2001 budget request, the FY 2001 education support allocation will be $41,202 per resident, about 5 percent less than the FY 1997 level. This reduction is occurring at the same time that per-resident costs could be increasing (according to findings from our literature review). The cause for this potential increase is a decline in the number of residents to bear the overhead costs of operating a program and the shift in training to ambulatory settings.

The VISNs allocate education support costs to the facilities based on network-wide considerations and using various methodologies. Some VISNs pass the funds directly through; others, particularly those that incorporate historical funding into their allocation formula, make no distinction between education and patient care costs.

Research Support ($331 million in FY 2001). The research support funds are allocated through VERA. These funds are intended to support clinical investigator salaries, research facilities, administrative costs, and patient care costs directly attributable to research that are not reimbursed by research funds. The funds are not included in the Basic and Complex Care allocations, because they are not related to patient workload. Unlike the education support funds, research support funds are passed directly to each medical center/care line/product line. Beginning in FY 2000, the allocation formula has been based on the level of total funded research. Data from the most recently ended fiscal year (as of the beginning of the allocation process) are used to determine allocations. For example, the FY 2001 allocations were calculated in FY 2000 using data from FY 1999. At the time that the calculations were being made in FY 2000, the data from FY 1999 were only a few months old. The funded amount is weighted by type of activity:

- VA-administered research, 100 percent;

- Non-VA-funded, non-VA-administered, peer-reviewed research, 75 percent; and,

- Non-VA-administered, non-peer-reviewed research, 25 percent.

The weighting is designed to improve reporting accountability and indirect cost recovery by rewarding VA-administered research. Consistent with our findings on educational activities, several sites mentioned that pressures for improved clinical productivity were making it more difficult to preserve protected time for research. The two-year interval between the funding of a research project and the flow of research support funds was also identified as problematic by a number of VISNs. The lapse necessitates finding other operational funds to support research projects that are starting up. We do not believe this should be as great a problem for VISNs that have a relatively stable, ongoing volume of research as it may be for VISNs that are trying to increase their research activities substantially. Although the research funds are not allocated through the VISN, the interviews showed that some VISNs take the research support funds into account when allocating other funds to the facilities. Thus, the availability of research support funds may reduce funding levels in other areas.

Recognition of Differences in Other Patient Care Costs

VERA includes no explicit adjustments for the potential effects that academic affiliations might have on other patient care costs after controlling for other factors such as case mix and geographic location.

- Operating fund allocations are based on the Basic and Complex Care categories. The labor adjustment assumes a standard staffing pattern but is weighted by the Basic and Complex Care categories.

- The equipment fund allocations include no case-mix adjustment.

Further analysis is needed to assess the appropriateness of these aspects of the allocation methodology. The basic issue is whether teaching-intensive facilities show systematic differences (relative to other facilities) that are not accounted for by the VERA methodology at the VISN level. It is closely related to the issue of case-mix refinement. Our analysis plan in Chapter 6 provides for an examination of the costs of maintaining academic affiliations within the context of an overall evaluation of VISN per capita costs. Currently, multiple funding streams support educational activities that affect service delivery and VISN financial performance. An evaluation of the net effect on costs should include all educational costs regardless of the source of funding used to support those costs. Otherwise, the analysis would not take into account both the cost of the educational activities and the value of the services provided in conjunction with those activities. We note that this type of analysis would not preclude establishing separate allocation methodologies for educational activities based on the results of that analysis. However, making a distinction between education support costs as they are currently defined and other costs of educational activity may be artificial. MedPAC's recommendation to combine the Medicare educational payments into a single supplemental payment is of great relevance to the VERA methodology. This relevance derives from the fact that, under VERA, physician compensation is included in both education support costs and other patient care costs, and the amounts reported as education support are based on teaching-physician compensation allocated for education support rather than on actual time spent in educational activities.

WHAT IS THE ROLE OF STATE-OF-THE-ART EQUIPMENT IN MAINTAINING ACADEMIC AFFILIATIONS AND THE RELATED COSTS?

Accreditation Requirements for Equipment

The Residency Review Committee (RRC) requirements related to equipment that must be available for resident training vary in specificity by specialty. For example, the RRC for internal medicine specifies that "facilities should be available to assure that residents become proficient in the effective use of current and evolving technologies" without enumerating specific technologies. The RRC requirements for ophthalmology accompany a general statement that "there must be access to current diagnostic equipment" with a detailed listing of the type of equipment that should be available. In contrast, the RRC requirements for general surgery do not explicitly address equipment needs (American Medical Association, 1999).

Generally, even where requirements are explicit, the intent is for the resident to receive training on state-of-the-art equipment over the course of the residency program. For most programs, the equipment does not need to be available at each resident training site. Thus, the importance of having state-of-the-art equipment at a particular VHA training facility depends on the capabilities of the other facilities participating in the residency program and the other VHA educational strengths. The types of services and patient mix at a particular VHA facility may be more important to the training program than access to the newest technologies. However, for a few procedure-intensive specialties, state-of-the-art equipment is a critical aspect of any training site. These programs include radiology, radiation oncology, and anesthesiology.

VERA Funding for Equipment Costs ($605 million in FY 2001)

From an accounting perspective, equipment costs fall into two basic categories: the costs of purchasing the equipment and the costs of operating the equipment. The latter involves the costs of training personnel to operate the equipment as well as ongoing operational costs, including associated personnel and medical supply costs. From an economic perspective, the equipment costs of affiliated VHA facilities should not be considered in isolation but rather as part of an overall evaluation of the effect of academic affiliations on patient care costs. We outline such an evaluation in Chapter 6.

Beginning in FY 2000, VERA funds for equipment purchases have been allocated to the VISNs based on patient workload. The allocation is not adjusted for case-mix differences; specifically, the allocation is based on the number of Complex, Basic Vested, and Basic Non-Vested patients served by each VISN. The equipment funds are allocated to each medical center/care line/product line based on networkwide considerations and needs. From our interviews with VISN staff, we concluded that patient care needs have the greatest weight in the allocation decisions. However, patient care needs and educational needs commonly overlap. The VHA facilities with major academic affiliations tend to be tertiary care facilities that function as referral centers within the VISNs. State-of-the-art equipment is frequently placed in these facilities so that veterans will have maximum access to the new technologies. Further, it was reported that the educational role of the affiliated hospital can be the deciding factor when a choice must be made between two facilities with similar levels of patient care need. In addition, affiliated facilities are able to benefit from shared service arrangements with non-VHA facilities.

VERA funding for the costs of operating state-of-the-art equipment is included in the allocations to the VISNs for Basic and Complex Care. Thus, the allocation for equipment operating costs is case-mix adjusted. The appropriateness of the allocation methodology needs to be considered as part of an overall evaluation of the effect of academic affiliations on facility costs. Even if equipment needs and costs are higher in facilities with major academic affiliations, offsetting cost reductions may arise through productivity gains or reductions in the overall cost of caring for certain patients.

SUMMARY OF FINDINGS

The VERA allocation methodology accounts for the costs directly associated with research and educational activities through the education support and research support funds. Overall, the methodologies used to allocate these funds appear reasonable.

With respect to education support funds, the number of residents correlates well with other health care trainees and is a straightforward allocation statistic. Our literature review identified a potential issue concerning the extent to which the size of the teaching program or level of teaching intensity might affect per-resident education support costs. This is an issue that would benefit from empirical analysis.

With respect to research support funds, we found general agreement with the allocation methodologies. Some concerns were voiced over the difficulty of supporting new research between the time the project starts and when the research support funds are allocated. However, some delay is unavoidable if funded research in a prior period is used as the allocation statistic.

With respect to the equipment needs associated with maintaining academic affiliations, we found that the importance of having state-of-the-art equipment depends on the RRC accreditation requirements and the resources of the other teaching sites. The VHA facilities with major affiliations generally benefit as referral centers in the equipment fund allocations from the VISNs. The costs of both purchasing and operating equipment should be considered in an overall evaluation of the effects of academic affiliations on costs.

The net costs of academic affiliations on VISN financial performance are difficult to measure since education, research, and patient care occur simultaneously. In addition to the costs that the education and research support funds are intended to cover, academic affiliations can involve other patient care costs such as those attributable to patient severity that are not measured by the case-mix system and more resource-intensive practice patterns. However, there are also benefits that need to be considered, including the value of the services provided by residents. While VERA takes research and education support costs into account, VERA does not explicitly consider the effects that maintaining academic affiliations may have on other patient care costs. As a result, there are potential issues related to the net effect of teaching and research on patient care costs and facility financial performance. These issues are closely related to issues involving case-mix measurement and are of concern only if they result in cost differences at the VISN level.

Currently, multiple funding streams support educational activities that affect service delivery and VISN financial performance. In examining the net effect of maintaining academic affiliations, all educational costs regardless of the source of funding used to support them should be included. The current distinction between education support costs and other patient care costs may be artificial because residents provide patient care services. Also, the impact of academic affiliations should not be examined independently but in conjunction with other factors that may affect costs.

During our study, we identified issues related to education and research that we believe are important but outside the scope of this study. These issues include the current distribution of funded residency positions, the impact of salary limitations on physician hiring, and the effect of overall funding levels on protected teaching and research time.

Chapter Five

VERA AND WEATHER-RELATED COSTS

A key congressional concern regarding the impact of VERA focuses on the degree to which the allocation system accounts for weather-related expenses. Theoretically, at least, VISNs in harsher climates might incur greater costs due to weather extremes. We addressed two specific questions central to this concern:

- To what degree does VERA account for cost differences across the VISNs that can be attributed to differences in weather?

- Should the VERA methodology be adjusted to account for any systematic differences in weather-related costs?

CONSIDERATIONS

In addressing these questions, we identified four dimensions of the weather issue that warrant consideration. These dimensions included building and maintenance costs, access to care, seasonal migration, and case mix.

First, weather differences experienced across the VISNs may lead to significant differences in the cost of building and maintaining facilities. For instance, facilities located in the northeastern, midwestern, and north central regions of the country may incur higher heating expenses in the winter than facilities located in regions where the weather is more moderate. Similarly, facilities located in the southeastern and southwestern regions may experience higher air-conditioning costs than facilities located elsewhere. In addition to these systematic differences in energy use patterns (and potential costs), the overwhelming majority of facilities are subject to some type of random, extreme weather events, such as hurricanes, tornadoes, floods, or blizzards. Finally, it is possible that facilities located in harsh weather climates (or in regions that experience comparably catastrophic non-meteorological events such as earthquakes) incur higher construction and maintenance costs, apart from energy use, than facilities located in other areas of the country.

The second dimension of the weather issue relates to the extent to which access to care on the part of veterans may be impeded by poor weather conditions. That is, do VISNs and facilities located in harsh weather areas incur certain expenses to ensure that veterans' access to care remains high even in the wake of extreme weather conditions or events? For example, do VISNs in these areas have to maintain a more costly distribution of clinics and services, transportation infrastructures, and staffing patterns than do other VISNs?

The third dimension focuses on the potential contribution of harsh weather in the northern regions of the country to significant fluctuations in patient volume due to the "snowbird" effect.

The final dimension that we considered focuses on case-mix differences across regions or facilities that are attributable to weather differences. For example, extreme heat can lead to increases in the number of patients seen for heat exhaustion, cardiovascular problems, and so on. Extreme cold weather coupled with heavy precipitation can lead to an increased incidence of hypothermia, accidents, and myocardial infarctions.

VERA'S ACCOUNTABILITY FOR WEATHER-RELATED COST DIFFERENCES

Although the current VERA methodology does not contain an explicit adjustment for any geographic differences in weather-related costs, it does provide several mechanisms to account for such cost differences.[1]

First, as indicated previously, Specific Purpose funds are set aside to cover contingencies that may arise during the course of the fiscal year. One such contingency could conceivably be an extreme weather event such as a hurricane or a tornado. VISN directors who serve an area that experiences an extreme weather event and incurs costs directly related to the event may apply to receive supplemental funding. It should also be noted that at the VISN level, reserve funds, which typically account for 1–2 percent of a VISN's budget, can also be used to cover the costs of weather-related shocks.

A second way in which the current methodology takes weather differences into account is by adjusting nonrecurring maintenance (NRM) expenses by the Boeckh Index. Published by Marshall & Swift/Boeckh, this index provides a measure of the relative cost of building new spaces or renovating existing ones. The index covers 11 building types and 115 cost elements—including 19 building trades, 89 types of materials, and 7 tax and insurance rates—for 203 U.S.

---

[1] The VA's Geographic Price Adjustment Workgroup has considered, but thus far has chosen not to recommend, adjusting VISN allocations to reflect energy cost differences.

cities. To the extent that the costs of labor, materials, insurance, and other construction costs are influenced by weather conditions, allocations made to VISNs to cover NRM costs will in fact be adjusted to reflect the differential impact of weather conditions.

ADJUSTING THE CURRENT VERA METHODOLOGY TO ACCOUNT FOR WEATHER-RELATED COSTS

Although the VERA methodology currently makes some adjustment for weather-related cost differences and provides mechanisms by which VISNs and facilities can obtain some financial relief from extreme weather events, the question arises as to whether these mechanisms are sufficient to account for weather-related cost differences. In other words, is an explicit and systematic adjustment to the VERA allocations warranted, and would such an adjustment improve equity and efficiency?

Differences in Building and Maintenance Costs

At first glance, one might argue that an allocation adjustment is needed to reflect differences in energy costs across the VISNs. In reality, energy costs account for a relatively small proportion of the VISNs' budget, typically in the neighborhood of 1 or 2 percent. Moreover, the variance in energy costs across the regions has been less than 1 percent of the operating budgets (DVA, 2001). However, as we heard from staff at many networks and facilities, recent sharp increases in energy costs have been difficult to manage: staff at one VISN in the Northeast reported that energy costs now represent 3–5 percent of their budget. Thus, energy costs are now a more substantial factor than in previous years. Moreover, while short-term spikes in energy prices, especially if such spikes were confined to a relatively small number of VISNs, could in principle be covered through the supplemental funding process, persistent cross-sectional differences in energy prices would argue for an energy price adjustment to the VERA allocations.

From a larger perspective, adjusting allocation rates to account for differences in energy costs poses several potential problems. First, because energy costs are the product of the number of units consumed times the price per unit, adjusting allocation rates on the basis of energy costs could reduce VISN and facility incentives to invest in energy-conserving technologies and programs such as the Energy Savings Performance Contracts (ESPC) to improve energy efficiency. Thus, any energy adjustment should be based on fuel and utility prices.

Second, a proposed energy price adjustment begs the question of whether adjustments should be made to reflect geographic differences in prices paid for other nonlabor inputs (such as food, laundry, pharmaceutical products, insurance, etc.).[2] Failing to adjust the allocations to reflect geographic differences in the prices paid for other inputs—and possibly other exogenous factors—while making such an adjustment for energy prices might compromise the degree to which the VERA system is perceived as being fair and equitable. At the same time, making a myriad of adjustments for nonlabor inputs could compromise VHA's goal of keeping the system as simple as possible, in terms of being understandable and easy to administer.

From a policy perspective, one could argue that adjusting VISN allocations to reflect geographic differences in nonlabor inputs is desirable. Toward that end, we recommend investigating the degree to which prices for all major nonlabor inputs vary geographically, developing an index that provides a valid and reliable aggregate measure of such variation, and testing the degree to which VISN and facility operating costs are affected by variation in nonlabor inputs. The recommended study is described further in Chapter 6.

Understanding the impact of weather on facility maintenance costs other than energy is a complicated matter. The real issue is whether facilities located in harsh weather environments incur systematically higher maintenance costs than facilities located in areas with less severe weather. It is quite possible that many of these differences will cancel each other out. For example, snow removal costs in the northern areas of the country may be balanced by mowing and watering costs in the South and West. In addition, roof maintenance in areas of the country that experience freeze-thaw cycles might be balanced by fungal damage in hot, humid environments, as reported by the staff at one facility in the South. However, the difficulty is in measuring these cost differences. Examining cost reports may fail to reveal true cost differences if the amounts actually expended by facilities fall short of the amounts needed to keep facilities in good repair. In other words, according to several of the interviews we conducted, facilities located in harsh weather climates sometimes use funds allocated for NRM to fund operations.[3] Therefore, the NRM figures recorded on the cost reports may misrepresent the actual maintenance needs of these facilities. To generate insight into this issue, a series of engineering studies comparing the maintenance needs of a sample of facilities located throughout the country may have to be undertaken.

---

[2] Interestingly, the Health Care Financing Administration has decided not to adjust Medicare reimbursement rates for geographic variation in nonlabor input prices.

[3] Ironically, devoting an inadequate level of resources to maintenance in the short run may lead to higher energy use, and therefore costs, as well as higher long-run maintenance costs.

Access to Care

With respect to the impact of harsh weather on access to care, most of the individuals interviewed believed that weather had no significant effects. That is, while some interviewees reported that inclement weather might lead to appointment cancellations and the need to engage in a substantial amount of rescheduling, no one argued that significant costs were associated with these activities. Interestingly, several of the interviews revealed that the growth of CBOCs in recent years—which is at least partly attributable to the incentives created under VERA—has actually served to minimize the impact of poor weather on access to care, because many veterans are no longer required to travel great distances when the roads are bad. Similarly, our review of the relevant literature revealed no evidence that would justify adjusting VISN allocations to account for systematic differences in access to care due to weather considerations.

In terms of the "snowbird" effect, our interviews revealed a mixed picture. VISN directors in the Sunbelt claim that a significant influx of patients occurs from the North during the winter months, although they also report believing that an increasing number of veterans are becoming full-year residents, which reduces somewhat the seasonal fluctuation in volume. However, VISN directors in the North do not report significant declines in patient volume over the winter months. This observation may be related in part to a higher incidence of cold weather–related illnesses such as flu and pneumonia that contribute to maintaining the usual patient census. It is important to note that VERA accounts for patient migration across VISN boundaries by prorating the amounts allocated for these patients on the basis of actual costs incurred. However, a potential problem regarding the prorated system mentioned in interviews is that patients who receive care from facilities located in two VISNs, for example, may be inherently more costly to treat than patients receiving care within a single VISN. This increase in costs may be due to factors such as the duplication of tests and the need to take multiple patient histories. VISNs in the northern regions also report that veterans who are "snowbirds" in their early retirement years tend to return to the North to be with their families in their later years when they require long-term and often costly care. Ultimately, the effect of patient migration is not known; it is an empirical question and one that could be addressed through the modeling approach outlined in Chapter 6.

Influence of Weather on Case Mix

Both our reviews of the relevant literature and our interviews results indicated that inclement weather can and does affect case mix. Broadly speaking, climatic conditions and changes in those conditions can be expected to influence the types and incidence of morbidity, as well as the extent to which the changes in morbidity affect various demographic groups and parts of the country (Longstreth, 1999; Patz, Engelberg, and Last, 2000; Patz et al., 2000). For example, extremes of temperature are closely correlated with certain morbidity and mortality patterns (Gaffen and Ross, 1998; Kalkstein and Davis, 1989; Kalkstein, 1993; Kilbourne, 1998; Rogot and Padgett, 1976).

Most published studies on climate and case mix are small-scale ones that typically address the impact of a single weather-related event over a short time period. Several of these studies have documented an increased use of emergency room services (Blindauer et al., 1999; Centers for Disease Control and Prevention, 1999a; Christoffel, 1985; Geehr et al., 1989) or increased hospital admissions (Semenza et al., 1999) on the part of patients presenting with weather-induced illnesses or accidents. A number of other studies examined the impact of a severe weather event on morbidity and mortality in a local area (Centers for Disease Control and Prevention, 1999b; Glass and Zack, 1979; Jones et al., 1982; Wainwright et al., 1999).

Interestingly, while we were able to identify studies, including those referenced above, that documented increased health services utilization during or immediately following a bout of bad weather, we failed to identify any studies that estimated the health system costs associated with such events. However, one article presented estimates of damage to various health facilities that resulted from a hurricane or tornado (Teschke, 1989).

In short, the results of several published studies and our own interviews tell us that weather—in terms of systematic differences in temperature and precipitation and extreme/unpredictable weather events—can be expected to have some effect on a facility's, and perhaps a VISN's, case mix. With respect to case-mix changes due to extreme and unpredictable weather events, any extraordinary costs incurred by a facility or VISN should be covered through the supplemental funding process. With respect to modifying VERA to account for systematic differences in case mix due to weather patterns across the country, this modification can best be accomplished by simply adopting a more refined case-mix measure than the one currently found in VERA.

SUMMARY OF FINDINGS

From a policy perspective, based on the review of the literature and on our interviews, we find no justification for adjusting VISN allocations directly to account for weather-related cost differences. Rather, we believe that the VA should investigate the extent to which prices of all nonlabor inputs vary geographically, with an eye toward making appropriate allocation adjustments, should there prove to be a significant amount of variation. Additionally, as stated above, any case-mix differences linked to weather could probably be handled through a comprehensive case-mix adjustment, rather than one that is simply targeted to weather-related conditions and procedures. An assessment of the extent of any misallocation and design of a comprehensive method to account for variations would require further empirical analysis.

Chapter Six

ANALYSIS PLAN FOR EVALUATING POTENTIAL VERA MODIFICATIONS

In the preceding three chapters, we identified a number of critical issues that emerged during the course of our study that we believe warrant additional consideration. As we have suggested, these issues can best be addressed through a quantitative analysis of various data sets maintained by the VA and residing at the Allocation Resource Center (ARC). In this chapter, we describe our recommended approach for studying the impact and potential value of modifications that might be made to VERA to address these issues.

It is important to recognize that the recommended analysis is not merely an academic exercise. Rather, it is designed to be policy relevant in two respects. First, it addresses a set of issues that are focused on enhancing the VA's ability to meet VERA's objectives. Second, it produces a tool and a set of results that can be translated immediately into changes in the ways in which resources are allocated to VISNs.

An underlying concern of the study described in this report, and one that was articulated in the legislation calling for this study, was whether the VERA system omitted certain factors in allocating resources. Specifically, these were factors important for ensuring veterans' access to VA services that had a predictable and systematic impact on the costs of providing health care to veterans, and that were largely outside the control of VISN directors.

With this concern in mind, we used three principles, or criteria, for determining the shape of the recommended analysis. First, the analysis had to be structured so as to yield clear, policy-relevant, practical recommendations for VERA. Second, the analytical approaches used had to be methodologically sound; in particular, they had to account for both individual- and facility-level characteristics. Third, the analysis had to be designed to incorporate the VA's overall mission for providing health care to veterans as well as the specific objectives of VERA—in particular, those related to equity and simplicity.

The analysis contained in this report revealed four general factors that we believe require additional analysis and that can be addressed in a way that meets the above criteria, namely,

- the health status of the population served (i.e., case mix);

- the teaching and research activities of each VA medical facility;

- physical plant characteristics, including the age of the facility, its size relative to the population it serves, its historical significance (if any), and any special maintenance needs; and

- geographic price variation in nonlabor inputs (e.g., energy, food, medical supplies, and pharmaceuticals).

UNITS OF ANALYSIS

The recommended study of potential modifications to the current VERA allocation methodology requires data to be analyzed at three levels:

- Veteran: because VERA is fundamentally a capitation-based allocation system, it is important to examine the annual costs generated by individual veterans in comparison to payment under both the current and alternative systems;

- Facility: many of the issues raised in the course of the study and presented in this report involve the characteristics of individual VA facilities—e.g., weather conditions, consolidation of facilities, and medical education. Thus, the impact of such characteristics on costs should be studied;

- VISN: ultimately, VERA is used to allocate resources to VISNs. As a result, it is critical to assess the impact of any change on total VISN allocations. VERA modifications have limited value if they increase the system's complexity while doing little to change resource allocations at the VISN level, even if they "improve" VERA's ability to explain the variation in individual costs.

The recommended analysis will enable the integration of the individual, facility, and VISN levels in an evaluation of VERA and potential modifications.

DATA REQUIREMENTS

To accomplish the planned analysis, we recommend that the ARC be assigned responsibility for creating the primary data sets to be used in the analysis. Prior to creation of these data sets, alternative risk adjustment approaches should be reviewed to determine whether any potentially useful approaches have not yet been evaluated by the DVA. The staff conducting the analysis would then have to consult extensively with the ARC during the construction of the data files to answer questions and address any issues that may arise. The central data set would be an annual, veteran-level cost file that is conceptually similar to the one that the ARC already creates and that would be combined with a series of additional individual-level variables. This file should include

- each veteran's annual VA costs, based on the veteran's VA health care use. Costs should be assigned to units of service based on facility-specific data, i.e., data that reflect the true cost of providing care at the specific facility (or facilities) where each veteran received the services. In the remainder of this chapter, "facility" denotes a reporting entity with a single budget, even if it includes structures in more than one physical location.

- each veteran's health status (risk adjustment) indicators, including the current three-category system and those systems stemming from the studies currently being undertaken, such as a modified DCG system. We would suggest the inclusion of risk-adjustment categories derived from several alternative risk-adjustment approaches so that they might be evaluated comprehensively as part of the suggested study.

- demographic and socioeconomic factors such as age, sex, reason(s) for VA eligibility, highest attained priority category, and zip code of primary residence.

- the facility identifiers for each VA facility where the veteran received care during the year and the fraction of care received at each facility (based on the prorated persons currently used by the VERA system to allocate veterans to VISNs if the veteran used more than one VISN in a given year).

- socioeconomic indicators for the veteran's zip code of residence; and measures of the availability of and travel distance to non-VA alternative medical facilities, based on the veteran's zip codes of residence. The former would be taken from census data and the latter from a variety of sources (such as the American Hospital Association Annual Survey of Hospitals and the Area Resource File; this element could be compiled by ARC or others).

Such data sets should be constructed for each year since the inception of the VERA system, if possible. Yearly data would allow the analysis to trace the responses to the implementation of the VERA system and to changes in the budgetary constraints over time.

In addition, the ARC should generate an annual facility-level file, covering each VA medical facility. This file should include facility characteristics such as facility type (for example, general acute care, tertiary care, long-term care, behavioral health), latitude and longitude, zip code, size, age, existence and intensity of involvement in education and research, range of services provided, and whether and when a consolidation occurred.

Finally, the ARC should characterize the budgetary implications of VERA to each VISN by providing their total budgets, deficits or surpluses, any supplemental requests, out-of-pocket or third-party collections, and carryovers for the last year prior to VERA and for all the subsequent years that will be analyzed.

PROPOSED ANALYSES

The discussion of the analysis plan is broken into two parts. We first provide a conceptual overview of the suggested analyses. We then provide a detailed technical description of the methodology that should be employed.

Conceptual Overview

The suggested analysis has three basic parts. The first stage focuses on estimating health care costs at the individual level, controlling for characteristics of the individual veteran. The second stage considers the impact of facility-specific characteristics on health care delivery costs. In the third stage, results from the individual- and facility-level models can be combined to generate estimates of total costs at the VISN level. The three-level structure of the analysis makes it possible to simulate how the allocation system as a whole would be affected by changes in any of the factors included in the model.

Individual-Level Analysis. This analysis would estimate the impact of an individual's characteristics (e.g., age, sex, and health status) on his or her total VA health care costs during the year. In addition, the individual-level cost model includes factors such as the availability of non-VA health care alternatives and the facility at which the patient received services, which could also have an impact on his or her health care costs. Estimates of the impact of the specific facility used on individual costs will be incorporated into the facility-level analysis as the dependent variable.

Facility-Level Analysis. Since there may be facility-specific characteristics that affect the cost of delivering health care, the second stage of the analysis estimates the impact of facility-level factors such as medical school affiliations, nonlabor prices, age of physical plant, and historic significance on facility-specific costs. Because this analysis uses the estimates of facility-specific costs from the individual-level analysis, the results provide information about the effects of facility characteristics while controlling for differences in the individual veterans that the facility serves.

VISN-Level Analysis. The results from the individual and facility-level analyses can be used to generate estimates of total costs at the VISN level by aggregating predicted expenditures. The analytical approach is designed to allow for estimating the impact of each characteristic (or group of characteristics) in isolation or in combination with others on annual costs. It is anticipated that a series of such analyses will be performed to identify the factors that are important in cost causation. Given its likely importance, we specifically recommend a review of potential risk adjustment approaches to identify ones that may be useful to the VA. This review should include the systems currently being evaluated by the VA but may extend to others. At this stage, simulations can be run to determine the impact of a change in any of the characteristics incorporated in the model on VISN costs. The results of these analyses would be reviewed with staff at VHA to construct VERA "scenarios" that represent potential changes to the VERA system. The financial effects of these scenarios would then be simulated and compared with the current system. We anticipate that this simulation model could provide a valuable planning tool with a variety of policy applications.

Technical Overview

Step 1: Individual-Level Analysis. The overall goal of the analyses is to evaluate the potential impact on health care costs of various veteran- and facility-level characteristics that may currently be excluded from VERA. We recommend beginning with a person-level multivariate model of annual VA health care costs, described in Equation 1. As we discuss further below, we recommend—for simplicity—first conducting analyses on the subset of veterans who utilized a single facility in the year (i.e., those whose prorated person value equals 1); in additional analyses, this restriction would be relaxed to test the robustness of the estimates.

Equation 1 would have the following general structure:

$$F(C_{ij}) = G(X_i'\beta_1 + H_i'\beta_2 + A_i'\beta_3 + S_j'\theta + \varepsilon_{ij})$$

(1)

where

C_{ij} is equal to the total annual costs for veteran i at facility j, determined using facility-specific costs as described above;

X_i is a vector of demographic and socioeconomic variables for veteran i;

H_i is a vector of health status (or risk adjustment) variables for veteran i;

A_i is a vector of availability of non-VA alternatives measures for veteran i;

S_j is a vector of dummy variables representing each VA facility; the jth in-
           dicator is 1, indicating that the veteran received services from facility j,
           and the remainder are 0;

ε_{ij} is an error that is i.i.d.$(0, \sigma^2)$; and

$\beta_1 - \beta_3$ and θ are parameters to be estimated.

In Equation 1, $F(\cdot)$ represents a transformation of the dependent variable, and $G(\cdot)$ represents the link function for the model. Annual health care costs are known to have a very skewed distribution, and it may be desirable to account for this skewness in the analyses; common methods include ordinary least squares regression with a log transformation of the dependent variable; and gamma regression with a log link.

A critical issue that this analysis would address is the implications of alternative health status/risk adjustment approaches. The VA is in the process of evaluating alternatives to the current three-category system (Basic Vested, Basic Non-Vested, and Complex Care). A separate model would be estimated with each of the alternative sets of health status categories derived from these risk adjustment approaches. One model would be based on the current system with three categories. Other sets would be based on other approaches that the VA is considering or have been identified through an initial survey of risk adjustment approaches. The initial group of multivariate regression models would enable comparison of the relative explanatory power of each set of health status categories controlling for all, some, or none of the other individual-level variables. For example, these models would allow for an assessment of whether demographic variables are useful in explaining the variation in costs in addition to health status measures or whether the variation in the accessibility of non-VA providers of care systematically affects VA costs.

In addition, each regression model would include a facility-specific constant for each VA facility. The constants represent the average facility-specific shift in costs after controlling for all the measurable veteran-level characteristics. Each model estimated with a different set of individual characteristics would generate a set of facility-specific constants. Similarly, estimates for each year would generate a separate set of these constants. This formulation recognizes that costs may depend on the characteristics of both the patient and the facility where he or she receives care. The facility-level effects are examined in additional detail in the second modeling stage, described below.

The costs to be generated will be used to study variations that are associated with different facility characteristics, *controlling for the characteristics of the veterans they serve.* Thus, it is essential that these costs are based on the application of accounting rules that are consistent across facilities and over time and that are based on parameters whose values depend solely on the output and experience of the individual facility in that year. The requirement for consistency and independence stems from the importance of the cost-accounting system for identifying site-specific effects (i.e., $\hat{\theta}$, the estimate of θ). Site-specific factors could affect veterans' costs in a number of ways, including changes in the volume of services each veteran uses, the mix of services, and the cost per unit of service. The methods used to assign costs to each service—which generates C_{ij}, total annual costs—should allow for all of these sources of cost variation to be reflected in $\hat{\theta}$.

As above, we recommend first focusing on veterans who used a single VA facility in the year, largely for ease of analysis. However, it will be important to test whether the results are sensitive to this restriction. For example, an initial test would involve examining the average characteristics (age, sex, eligibility status, health status) of the "single-facility" population and the "multiple-facility" one (veterans who used more than one facility in that year).

If, as expected, the populations look different, it would be necessary to test the robustness of the results from the "single-facility" analysis by performing a similar set of analyses on the entire population (single- and multiple-facility combined). The analysis will have the same basic structure except that the multiple-facility veterans will have more than one facility-specific constant associated with them. For such veterans, the facility identifier for each facility they used during the year will be multiplied by the corresponding prorated patient (PRP). A veteran who used only Facility$_1$ would have an indicator variable only for that facility associated with him or her (i.e., the Facility$_1$ indicator variable would have a value of 1, and all other facility indicator variables would have a value of 0). For a veteran whose costs were evenly split between Facility$_1$ and Facility$_2$, both Facility$_1$ and Facility$_2$ indicator variables would take on values of 0.5, and all other facility indicator variables would take on values of 0. Such a characterization implies that aside from the individual veteran's personal characteristics, the facility-specific shift in costs will depend equally on the two facilities.

The first test of robustness would be a comparison of the corresponding coefficients for a representative group of models. Statistical tests would be conducted to see if the coefficients estimated using the full population were statistically different from those based on the single-facility subpopulation. Any characteristic or set of characteristics that consistently differs between the full- and single-facility estimates would require further investigation. The robustness of the estimates would then require testing in the second, facility-level stage of the analysis.

Step 2: Facility-Level Analysis. The next stage of the analysis would use the vector of facility-specific average shifts in annual costs ($\hat{\theta}$, with elements $\hat{\theta}_j$) as dependent variables. Each version of the regression models estimated for individual veterans will have a set of facility-specific constants associated with it. Each of these sets of facility constants could then be related to a range of facility characteristics as the independent variables in a second-stage multivariate analysis. In these regression models, the estimated coefficients of a particular characteristic would measure its association, on average, with a shift in annual costs. This model would have the following general form:

$$F(\hat{\theta}_{jt}) = G(L'_{jt}\delta_1 + M'_{jt}\delta_2 + P'_{jt}\delta_3 + I'_{jt}\delta_4 + C'_{jt}\delta_5 + T'\delta_6 + v_j) \tag{2}$$

where

$\hat{\theta}_{jt}$ are the estimated facility-specific average shifts in annual costs, based on the results of Equation 1;

L_{jt} is a vector of location-related measures;

M_{jt} is a vector of medical affiliation measures;

P_{jt} is a vector of labor and nonlabor prices;

I_{jt} is a vector of measures of the physical plant/infrastructure;

C_{jt} is a vector of consolidation-related measures;

T is a set of year indicator variables;

v_j is an error that is i.i.d.$(0, \sigma^2)$; and

$\delta_1 - \delta_5$ are parameters to be estimated.

Once this model is estimated, one could then examine the relationship, for instance, between costs at VA facilities that have academic affiliations and those that do not. It is important to remember that the first and second stages are linked. For example, it is likely that the estimated impact of academic affiliations in the second stage will have a strong relationship with the specific set of health status measures used in the first stage. A more aggregate set of health status measures would likely show a much larger effect of affiliation than one that makes finer distinctions. This stage would allow for a test of alternative measures for these characteristics.

Using the affiliation example once again, one measure of educational intensity might be the ratio of residents and interns to beds. Other measures, such as one that simply distinguishes intense from marginal educational programs, could be tried as well. In addition, the importance of facility characteristics omitted from this model can be assessed by examining the proportion of total variation in these facility-specific cost shifts accounted for by the variables in the model. At this stage, one could test hypotheses as to whether facility characteristics, aside from those listed above, account significantly for variations in cost.

Once again, the robustness of the conceptually simple single-facility estimates of these constants will be tested with the values and the corresponding relationships for some complete population estimates.

Step 3: Aggregating to the VISN level. The analyses in Steps 1 and 2 will enable explicit evaluation of the impacts of including or excluding particular determinants of cost when determining VISN budgets under VERA. Specifically, once these analyses are completed, one could examine the parameter estimates to determine whether the hypothesized relationships between individual- and facility-level characteristics and costs are confirmed by the data. In doing so, we recommend that both the statistical and substantive significance of the parameter estimates be considered.

The third step of the proposed analysis involves using the parameter estimates from Equations 1 and 2 to predict costs for each veteran, controlling for different combinations of individual- and facility-level factors. To do so, one would first use the parameter estimates from Equation 2 $(\hat{\delta}_1 - \hat{\delta}_5)$ to calculate predicted facility-level shifters $(\hat{\theta}_j^*)$. One would then use the parameter estimates from Equation 1 $(\hat{\beta}_1 - \hat{\beta}_3)$ and the $\hat{\theta}_j^* s$ to predict annual costs (C_{ij}^*) for each veteran.

These cost estimates can be aggregated to the VISN level, and the results can be compared with the resources that each VISN would receive using the current VERA system.[1] Although we recognize that VERA is intended as a VISN-based system, one could also aggregate costs to the facility level and compare costs with the resources that each facility would receive. This comparison might provide useful reference information for VISN directors.

Simulating the Effects of Modifications to VERA

Based on the results of these analyses, it will be possible to make concrete analyses of plausible modifications to the current VERA system. The staff undertak-

---

[1] We recognize that the simulations will have to be subjected to a budget constraint that reflects the annual appropriation.

ing this analysis and VHA staff could then develop a series of potential VERA modifications and use the data to simulate the effects of such changes on VISN budgets. At this stage, we anticipate that a wide range of simulations is likely to be valuable both for planning purposes and to help refine VERA to meet its goals.

Finally, it should be noted that while the simulation results will provide critical information on possible VERA modifications, ultimately, policymakers will also have to consider whether any such modifications are consistent with VERA's goals and objectives.

We note one caveat that should be kept in mind when considering the proposed analyses. While VA facilities or VISNs may operate at different levels of efficiency, in general, it is difficult to identify definitively which organizations are operating relatively inefficiently. For example, hospitals may have different average occupancy rates for their beds, but within a fairly wide range, few objective guidelines exist for assessing whether the rate at a particular facility is inappropriate. We recommend that this issue be kept in mind in interpreting the results of empirical analyses. In some cases, it may also be valuable to identify facilities or VISNs that are outliers with respect to particular cost factors and investigate the possible reasons.

Chapter Seven

CONCLUSIONS

Our assessment of the VERA system focused on several critical issues identified by the Congress and the Department of Veterans Affairs:

- the impact of the VERA methodology on VISNs with relatively old medical facilities and those that care for patients who are older and/or more disabled than patients residing in other VISN service areas;

- the ability of VISNs to consolidate facilities and services;

- DVA medical center affiliations with university teaching and research hospitals; and

- the extent to which geographic differences in weather conditions—and the impact of those conditions on patients' access to care—are taken into account.

We addressed these issues largely through a review of previous studies of VERA and the relevant health services research literature as well as a series of interviews that we conducted at a sample of VISNs and VA medical facilities. Briefly, the results of our analysis led us to the following conclusions:

- Health care delivery costs may be affected by the age and physical condition of a VISN's capital infrastructure. Currently, VERA does not take these factors into account in determining VISN allocations. Thus, we recommend a quantitative analysis of this issue to determine the extent of such effects at the VISN level.

- The VA is currently considering using a DCG-based case-mix methodology in the future. Refining the current case-mix adjustment along these lines could represent an improvement to VERA.

- External pressure from key stakeholders presents a formidable barrier to efforts to consolidate facilities and services.

- VERA accounts for costs associated with maintaining academic affiliations through education support and research support allocations.

However, the net effect of teaching and research on patient care costs and facility financial performance has not been established. Our review of the literature raises potential questions regarding whether there are systematic differences between facilities with major affiliations and other facilities that would affect costs at the VISN level. These issues are closely related to issues involving case-mix measurement.

- With respect to equipment required for academic affiliations, we found from our interviews that facilities with major affiliations generally benefit as referral centers in the VISN equipment fund allocations. The costs of both purchasing and operating needed equipment should be investigated as part of an overall evaluation of the net effect of maintaining academic affiliations.

- From our review of the literature and our interviews, we find no clear reason for adjusting VISN allocations directly to account for weather-related cost differences. Rather, the VA should investigate the extent to which prices of all nonlabor inputs vary geographically, with an eye toward making appropriate allocation adjustments should the amount of variation prove to be significant.

- Any case-mix differences linked to weather should be accounted for through a comprehensive case-mix adjustment, rather than one that is simply targeted to weather-related conditions and procedures.

- It is important that any potential adjustment not be considered in isolation. Rather, adjustments should be considered in the broader context of a comprehensive health care delivery cost model.

Our study also yielded some important conclusions regarding the overall impact of VERA that do not fit neatly within the specific issues addressed. First, we found that VERA represents only one piece of the veterans' health care puzzle, albeit an important one. That is, in assessing the impact of VERA, one must always be cognizant that a broad range of factors influence the cost and manner in which health care is provided to the veteran population. Other critical factors include (but are not limited to) financial considerations, such as the size of the annual congressional VHA appropriation and the ways in which VISN directors allocate resources to individual facilities; the demographic characteristics and the health care needs of the veteran population; the availability of non-VA sources of care; and a myriad of political factors.

Second, we want to emphasize that in spite of VERA's possible shortcomings, we note that VERA appears to be designed to meet its objectives of reallocating resources to match the geographic distribution of the veteran population more closely. In addition, the overwhelming majority of interviewees indicated that

VERA was preferable to previous VA budget allocation systems in terms of its incentive structure, degree of fairness, and simplicity.

Third, we noted that VERA is being refined on a continuous basis. In fact, this study represents one in a series of approximately a half dozen that have been undertaken by external organizations since the system's inception less than five years ago. Moreover, nine work groups composed of representatives from the 22 VISNs are constantly monitoring various aspects of the system's operations and recommending modifications they deem appropriate. VHA has implemented many of the recommended changes contained in both the external evaluators' reports as well as the Workgroups' memoranda.

Fourth, a common concern among many of the VISN and facility directors interviewed is the lack of a geographic adjustment to the means test that is used to determine a veteran's financial status with regard to eligibility for services. Veterans without a service-connected disability whose annual incomes and net worth are above the established dollar threshold and are not in Complex Care fall into Priority Group 7c and are currently not included in VERA workload calculations. The threshold is the same for all regions of the country. Consequently, there are inequities in access to covered services for veterans in high-cost-of-living areas. In addition, VISNs lose out on potential VERA credit for veterans who are classified as Priority 7 but who would fall into Priority Group 5 if the means test was adjusted for geographic differences in the costs of living. VHA is well aware of this inequity; however, a change in the eligibility measures is not within their purview and would require congressional action.

Fifth, our analysis revealed that VERA could benefit from using a more sophisticated process to obtain workload estimates. Currently, VISN allocations for Basic Care are based on workload data that are generated by counting eligible veterans who used VA services during a three-year period. A model that incorporates, for instance, demographic characteristics and historical use patterns would yield a set of allocations that matches the VISNs' needs more closely. The VA has used actuarial projections of use and costs in their planning process but has not incorporated them into VERA, possibly because of the complexity associated with the underlying actuarial models. However, some complexity is necessary to obtain a more equitable distribution of resources.

Sixth, additional data should be collected and reported on contract services. VISN and facility directors frequently reported difficulty managing the cost of these services, especially in rural areas where the choice of providers is relatively slim. Unfortunately, cost data on contract services are typically presented as an aggregate number in facility cost reports, so it may not be possible to analyze the impact of various kinds of contract services on total facility costs or cost per case.

Significant additional insight into VERA can be gained through a quantitative analysis, along the lines described in Chapter 6, of several key data sets maintained by VHA. Because of the project's short time frame (six months), we were unable to undertake this analysis. Yet doing so would yield valuable information on the potential need for, and consequences of, various modifications to the VERA allocation system. Such modifications would include those related to case mix, geographic differences in the prices paid for nonlabor inputs (including energy prices and contract labor costs), teaching and research hospital affiliations, and the condition of facilities' physical plants. Such an analysis would constitute a logical extension of the VA's ongoing effort to ensure that VERA remains an efficient, effective, and equitable resource allocation system.

KEY FORMULAS AND DATA IN THE FY 2001 VERA

In addition to covering the costs associated with patient care, VERA allocated over $1.5 billion to the VISNs in FY 2001 to support research, education, equipment purchases, and NRM expenses. Research support allocations to the networks for FY 2001 were based on the amount of research funded in FY 1999. Education support is allocated on the basis of the number of approved residents. In contrast, equipment and NRM funds are allocated strictly on the basis of workload. The Boeckh Index, which is published by Marshall & Swift/Boeckh, is used to adjust NRM for geographic differences in construction costs. Table A.1 contains a description of the formulas used to allocate VERA funds in FY 2001.[1]

---

[1] DVA (2001).

Table A.1

Key Formulas and Data in the FY 2001 VERA

Allocation Factors	Total Dollars Allocated	Mechanism to Determine Total Dollars	Definitions of Workload (Unit of Measure)	National Total Workload (Unit of Measure)	National Price/ Allocation Rate
Basic Vested Care	$9,910,784,598	61.25 percent of Basic Care (Vested and Non-Vested) and Complex Care dollars. Percentage updated based on FY 1999 cost experience	Number of Basic Care patients in the three-year Cat A/X user file. Three-year file includes FYs 1997, 1998, and 1999 patients who rely on VA for their care. These patients have used inpatient services or have had an appropriate detailed medical evaluation during the past three years. Includes compensation and pension exam visits. Workload units based on historical utilization are adjusted to reflect care across networks.	3,170,651	$3,126 per basic workload unit
Basic Non-Vested Care	$52,655,120	0.32 percent of Basic Care (Vested and Non-Vested) and Complex Care dollars	Number of Basic Care patients in the three-year Cat A/X user file who use some VA health care services but are less reliant on the VA system. Excludes compensation and pension exam patients. Excludes all collateral visits. Workload units based on historical utilization are adjusted to reflect care across networks.	436,265	$121 per non-vested patient

Table A.1—continued

Allocation Factors	Total Dollars Allocated	Mechanism to Determine Total Dollars	Definitions of Workload (Unit of Measure)	National Total Workload (Unit of Measure)	National Price/ Allocation Rate
Complex Care	$6,217,422,282	38.42 percent of Basic Care (Vested and Non-Vested) and Complex Care dollars (same percent as previous years)	Number of Complex Care patients forecasted to use the VISN in FY 2001. This one-year forecasted number is based on historical utilization over five years (FYs 1995–1999). Workload units based on historical utilization are adjusted to reflect care across networks. REVISED: The forecast continues to include a factor for age, but no longer for veteran population trends.	145,385	$42,765 per complex workload unit
Geographic price adjustment	$0	The geographic price adjustment (labor index) is applied against $10.1 billion labor dollars expended in FY 1999.	The FY 2001 VERA labor index is computed using four pay periods of FY 1999 normal pay data only and using a national market basket approach. For FY 2001, the labor index is computed using national-level staffing patterns versus VISN-level staffing, which was used prior to FY 2000. REVISED this year to weight the Complex Care workload.		

Table A.1—continued

Allocation Factors	Total Dollars Allocated	Mechanism to Determine Total Dollars	Definitions of Workload (Unit of Measure)	National Total Workload (Unit of Measure)	National Price/ Allocation Rate
Research support	$331,144,000	Total of research support dollars in the FY 2001 President's budget	Dollars of FY 1999 funded research (intra- and extramural research). Applies weights: 100 percent for VA-administered research; 75 percent for peer-reviewed research that is not VA administered; 25 percent for non-peer-reviewed research that is not VA administered.	$752,048,377 unweighted; $633,475,448 weighted	$0.52 per dollar of reported funded research
Education support	$356,894,000	Total of education support dollars in the FY 2001 President's budget	Number of residents for academic year 2000/2001	8,662	$41,202 per resident
Subtotal	$16,868,900,000				
Equipment-capitation	$605,047,000	Total of equipment dollars in the FY 2001 Medical Care budget	The Equipment allocation is based totally on workload (Sum of Basic Vested, Basic Non-Vested, and Complex Care workload)	3,752,301 prorated patients (PRPs) (Basic Vested, Basic Non-Vested plus Complex Care PRPs)	$161

Table A.1—continued

The revised NRM model was phased in over three years. In FY 2001, the NEW MODEL is fully implemented.

Allocation Factors	Total Dollars Allocated	Mechanism to Determine Total Dollars	Definitions of Workload (Unit of Measure)	National Total Workload (Unit of Measure)	National Price/ Allocation Rate
NRM-Boeckh Index times total workload NEW MODEL	$272,463,000	Derived from nonrecurring maintenance dollars in the FY 2001 Medical Care budget	NEW MODEL: In FY 2001, the NRM allocation is totally based on workload adjusted by the Boeckh Index (Workload [PRPs] times Boeckh Index). This Boeckh Index, which is an external inflation index that measures the relative cost of building and/or renovating space, is no longer adjusted by the square footage, age, and number of buildings.	68,272 units—sum of [Network, PRPs times Network Boeckh Index]	$3,991
Total capital amounts	$877,510,000	Derived from FY 2001 Medical Care budget			
Total $ General Purpose	$17,746,410,000	Derived from FY 2001 Medical Care budget less Specific Purpose funding			

GUIDE FOR RAND VERA SITE VISITS—NETWORKS

RAND's study of the Veterans Equitable Resource Allocation (VERA) System Methodology will include site visits to the Allocation Resource Center, the DVA Headquarters, and various VISNs and facilities across the country. The purpose of visiting network centers is to determine how VERA impacts the way in which the networks function. Specifically, how does VERA impact patient care services, financial performance, medical education, and research across the network? In addition, what key variables could be included in the VERA methodology to reflect cost differences associated with (1) facility age; (2) patient age, comorbidities, level of disability, and functional status; (3) VISN restructuring/consolidation; (4) geographic location (urban/rural, weather conditions, etc.); (5) capacity concerns (e.g., occupancy rates, waiting time for appointments, etc.); (6) degree of affiliation with medical schools and research institutions; and (7) other factors that may have an impact on costs (e.g., managed care penetration rates)?

1. Network Demographics and Environment

- Size of the network and average distance patients travel to receive care (inpatient/outpatient)

- What are the civilian alternatives for care and do patients use both systems?

- What are the annual Medical Care Cost Fund (MCCF) collections?

- Unique characteristics of patients in this network

  —Age: percent 56–75; percent over 75

  —Severity of illness, level of disability, special health care needs

- Does the rural/urban environment of the network impact

  —the range of services provided?

  —the costs of delivering services?

  —patient accessibility or recruitment?

- Does the network experience harsh weather conditions (extreme heat and/or humidity, extreme cold, significant snowfall) for three or more months during the year? What are the effects of harsh weather on

   —delivery of health care services

    - types of illnesses/accidents

    - inpatient and ER utilization

    - patient accessibility

    - missed appointments

   —energy costs

   —maintenance/construction costs

- What is the condition of the physical plant facilities across the network with regard to age, need for renovation, maintenance costs, historical landmark status, etc.?

2. History

- How were prior allocation systems better/worse for the network?

- Has the network received increased or decreased funding through VERA?

3. VISN/Facility Issues

- What is the organizational structure of the network (service lines)?

- What are the mechanisms for communication and feedback between the VISN and the facilities?

- How much consolidation has taken place (or is planned) within the VISN and what is the impact on the network with regard to delivery of services, staffing, etc.?

4. Methodology for allocation to facilities

- How are allocation decisions made?

- How has VERA affected allocations to the facilities?

- Which facilities have received increased funding since VERA and which have received decreased funding since VERA?

5. Impact of VERA

- How has VERA affected recruitment/retention of patients across the network?

- How has VERA affected recruitment/retention of staff across the network?
- How has VERA affected the mix of patients treated?
- How has VERA affected delivery of services for
  —Basic Care patients
  —Complex Care patients
- How has VERA affected Quality Improvement activities?
- How has VERA impacted the medical education and research programs across the network?
- What economic incentives are created by VERA at the network level?
- What economic incentives are created by VERA at the facility level?

6. Benefits of VERA to the VISN

7. Drawbacks of VERA to the VISN

8. What changes has the network made in the past four years to improve efficiency and decrease costs?

9. Suggestions for changes to VERA

GUIDE FOR RAND VERA SITE VISITS—FACILITIES

RAND's study of the Veterans Equitable Resource Allocation (VERA) System Methodology will include site visits to the Allocation Resource Center, the DVA Headquarters, and various VISNs and facilities across the country. The purpose of visiting facilities is to determine how VERA impacts the way in which facilities do business. Specifically, how does VERA impact patient care services, financial performance, medical education, and research at the facility level? In addition, what key variables could be included in the VERA methodology to reflect cost differences associated with (1) facility age; (2) patient age, comorbidities, level of disability, and functional status; (3) VISN restructuring/consolidation; (4) geographic location (urban/rural, weather conditions, etc.); (5) capacity concerns (e.g., occupancy rates, waiting time for appointments, etc.); (6) degree of affiliation with medical schools and research institutions; and (7) other factors that may have an impact on costs (e.g., managed care penetration rates)?

1. Facility Demographics and Environment

- Size of catchment area and average distance patients come to receive care (inpatient/outpatient)

- Does the catchment area overlap with other VA facilities?

- What are the civilian alternatives for care and do patients use both systems?

- What are the annual MCCF collections?

- Unique characteristics of patients utilizing this facility

    —Age: percent 56–75; percent over 75

    —Severity of illness, level of disability, special health care needs

- What is the status of the physical plant (age, need for update, maintenance costs, historical landmark status, etc.)?

- Clinic wait times

—What is the average time a patient must wait for a clinic appointment?

—What percentage of patients wait 45 days or more for an appointment?

—Do clinic wait times vary over the course of the year?

- Provider wait times

—What is the average time a patient must wait to see the provider?

—What percentage of patients wait longer than 25 minutes to see the provider?

- Does the rural/urban environment of the facility impact

—the range of services provided?

—the costs of delivering services?

—patient accessibility or recruitment?

- Does the facility experience harsh weather conditions (extreme heat and/or humidity, extreme cold, significant snowfall) for three or more months during the year? What are the effects of harsh weather on

—delivery of health care services

- types of illnesses/accidents
- inpatient and ER utilization
- patient accessibility
- missed appointments

—Energy costs

—Maintenance/construction costs

2. History

- How has the creation of VISNs affected the facility?
- What were the benefits/drawbacks of earlier resource allocation methods?

3. VISN/Facility Issues

- How does network organization affect the facility (service lines)?
- What are the mechanisms for communication and feedback between the VISN and the facility?
- How much consolidation has taken place (or is planned) within the VISN and what is the impact on the facility with regard to delivery of services, staffing, etc.?

- What is the current methodology for allocating resources from the VISN to the facility?

4. Impact of VERA

- What financial impact has VERA had on the facility? (Increased or decreased funding?)

- How has VERA affected your recruitment/retention of patients?

- How has VERA affected your recruitment/retention of staff?

- How has VERA affected the mix of patients treated?

- How has VERA affected delivery of services for

  —Basic Care patients

  —Complex Care patients

- How has VERA affected facility Quality Improvement activities?

- How has VERA impacted the medical education and research programs at the facility?

- How has VERA affected physical plant maintenance?

5. What incentives are created by VERA?

6. What are the overall benefits of VERA to the facility?

7. What are the major drawbacks of VERA to the facility?

8. What changes has the facility made in the past four years to increase efficiency and decrease costs?

9. Suggestions for changes to VERA

VERA ELIGIBILITY CATEGORIES AND PRIORITY GROUPS

WHAT ARE THE PRIORITY GROUPS AND CATEGORIES?

The Priority Groups define the order of priority for VERA enrollment. These groups are numbered 1 through 7, with 1 conferring the highest priority for enrollment. Priority Group 7 is divided into two subgroups, a and c (see below). Priority Groups 1 through 6 and 7a are also defined as Category A in the VERA Basic Care component. Priority Group 7c is defined as Category C.

Priority Group 1

- Veterans with service-connected disabilities rated 50 percent or more disabling

Priority Group 2

- Veterans with service-connected disabilities rated 30 percent or 40 percent disabling

Priority Group 3

- Veterans who are former POWs

- Veterans whose discharge was for a disability that was incurred or aggravated in the line of duty

- Veterans with service-connected disabilities rated 10 percent or 20 percent disabling

- Veterans awarded special eligibility classification under Title 38, U.S.C., Section 1151, "Benefits for individuals disabled by treatment or vocational rehabilitation"

Priority Group 4

- Veterans who are receiving aid and attendance or housebound benefits
- Veterans who have been determined by VA to be catastrophically disabled

Priority Group 5

- Veterans with nonservice-connected disabilities and veterans with service-connected injuries/illnesses who are rated 0 percent disabled, whose annual income and net worth are below the established dollar threshold

Priority Group 6

- All other eligible veterans who are not required to make copayments for their care, including

  —World War I and Mexican Border War veterans

  —veterans receiving care solely for disabilities resulting from exposure to toxic substances or radiation or for disorders associated with service in the Gulf War; or for any illness associated with service in combat in a war after the Gulf War or during a period of hostility after November 11, 1998

  —veterans with service-connected injuries who are considered 0 percent disabled but qualify for compensation (compensable)

Priority Group 7

- Veterans in Priority Group 7 have income and net worth at or above established income level and are expected to pay a specified copayment
- 7a—Veterans who do not fall into any of the above groups, whose illness/injury is service related but who are not entitled to compensation, because they are 0 percent disabled; also included in this group are veterans who receive compensation and pension exams. Priority Group 7a veterans are classified as Category A patients in the VERA Basic Care component
- 7c—Veterans whose illness/injury is non-service connected. 7c veterans form Category C and are not included in the VERA Basic Care component

Alexander, J. A., M. T. Halpern, and S.Y.D. Lee, "The Short-Term Effects of Merger on Hospital Operations," *Health Services Research*, Vol. 30, No. 6, 1996, pp. 827–847.

Allocation Resource Center (ARC), *VERA 2000 Veterans Equitable Resource Allocation System ARC Technical Manual*, 2000.

AMA Systems, Inc., The Center for Naval Analysis Corporation, "Evaluation of Rural Health Care in the 22 Veterans Integrated Service Networks," Contract No. V101 (93) P-1502 Task Order 17, March 2000.

AMA Systems, Inc., The Center for Naval Analysis Corporation, "Evaluation of Patient Health Status by VISN: Final Report," Contract No. V101 (93) P-1502 Task Order 17, July 2000.

American Medical Association, *AMA Graduate Medical Education Directory 1998–1999*, Washington, D.C.: American Medical Association, 1999.

Anderson, D. M., and M. B. Hampton, "Physician Assistants and Nurse Practitioners: Rural-Urban Settings and Reimbursement for Services," *Journal of Rural Health*, Vol. 15, No. 2, 1999, pp. 252–263.

Anderson, G. F., and J. R. Lave, "Financing Graduate Medical Education Using Multiple Regression to Set Payment Rates," *Inquiry*, Vol. 23, Summer 1986, pp. 191–199.

Blindauer, K. M., C. Rubin, D. L. Morse, and M. McGeehin, "The 1996 New York Blizzard: Impact on Noninjury Emergency Visits," *American Journal of Emergency Medicine*, Vol. 17, 1999, pp. 23–27.

Boex, J. R., "Factors Contributing to Variability of Direct Costs for Graduate Medical Education in Teaching Hospitals," *Academic Medicine*, Vol. 67, No. 2, 1992, pp. 80–84.

Boex, J. R., R. Blacklow, A. Boll, L. Fishman, S. Gamliel, M. Garg, V. Gilchrist, A. Hogan, P. Meservey, S. Pearson, R. Politzer, and J. J. Veloski, "Understanding the Costs of Ambulatory Care and Training," *Academic Medicine*, Vol. 73, No. 9, 1998, pp. 943–947.

Bosanac, E. M., R. C. Parkinson, and D. S. Hall, "Geographic Access to Hospital Care: A 30-Minute Travel Time Standard," *Medical Care*, Vol. 14, 1976, pp. 616–624.

Bronstein, J. M., and M. A. Morrissey, "Determinants of Rural Travel Distance for Obstetrics Care," *Medical Care*, Vol. 28, 1990, pp. 853–865.

Campbell, C. R., K. N. Gillespie, and J. C. Romies, "The Effects of Residency Training Programs on the Financial Performance of Veterans Affairs Medical Centers," *Inquiry*, Vol. 28, 1991, pp. 288–299.

Center for Health Quality, Outcomes, and Economic Research, "Health Status and Outcomes of Veterans: Physical and Mental Component Summary Scores Veterans SF-36—1999 Large Health Survey of Veteran Enrollees Executive Report," Washington, D.C.: Office of Quality and Performance (10Q) Veterans Health Administration Department of Veterans Affairs, 2000.

Centers for Disease Control and Prevention, "Heat-Related Illnesses and Deaths—Missouri, 1998, and United States, 1979–1996," *Journal of the American Medical Association*, Vol. 282, No. 3, July 21, 1999a, pp. 227–228.

Centers for Disease Control and Prevention, "Surveillance of Morbidity During Wildfires—Central Florida, 1998," *Morbid Mortal Weekly Report*, Vol. 48, No. 4, 1999b, pp. 78–79.

Christoffel, K. K., "Effect of Season and Weather on Pediatric Emergency Department Use," *American Journal of Emergency Medicine*, Vol. 3, 1985, pp. 327–330.

Commonwealth Fund, "New Approaches to Academic Health Center Affiliations: Public Hospitals and the Department of Veterans Affairs," Issue Brief, April 1999.

Council on Graduate Medical Education, "Fifteenth Report: Financing Graduate Medical Education in a Changing Health Care Environment," Rockville, Md.: Department of Health and Human Services, 2000.

Council on Graduate Medical Education, "Physician Distribution and Health Care Challenges in Rural and Inner City Areas," 10th Report, Washington, D.C.: U.S. Government Printing Office, 1998.

Cromley, E., and G. W. Shannon, "Locating Ambulatory Medical Care Facilities for the Elderly," *Health Services Research*, Vol. 21, 1986, pp. 499–514.

Dalton, K., and E. C. Norton, "Revisiting Rogowski and Newhouse on the Indirect Costs of Teaching: A Note on Functional Form and Retransformation in Medicare's Payment Formulas," *Journal of Health Economics*, Vol. 19, No. 16, 2000, pp. 1027–1047.

Dalton, K., E. C. Norton, and K. Kilpatrick, "A Longitudinal Study of the Effects of Graduate Medical Education on Hospital Operating Costs," *Health Services Research*, Vol. 35, No. 6, 2001, 1267–1291.

Department of Health and Human Services, "Medicare Program—Prospective Payment System for Hospital Outpatient Services: Proposed Rules," *Federal Register*, Vol. 63, No. 173, 1998, p. 47581.

Department of Veterans Affairs, "Report of Residency Realignment Review Committee," submitted to the Under Secretary for Health, May 7, 1996.

Department of Veterans Affairs Education Model Workgroup, "Indirect Medical Education Support Model," issue paper, undated.

Department of Veterans Affairs Office of Academic Affiliations, "Graduate Medical Education Realignment. Strategies for Meeting VHA's Goals for Graduate Medical Education Realignment," http://www.va.gov/OAA/docs/GMEDocs/General/Article_GME_PCSTRAT3.asp, last accessed May 29, 2000.

Department of Veterans Affairs, Veterans Health Administration, *VERA—Veterans Equitable Resource Allocation: Equity of Funding and Access to Care Across Networks*, 5th ed., Washington, D.C.: March 2001.

Gaffen, D. J., and R. J. Ross, "Increased Summertime Heat Stress in the U.S.," *Nature*, Vol. 396, December 10, 1998, pp. 529–530.

Geehr, E. C., R. Salluzzo, S. Bosco, J. Braaten, T. Wahl, and V. Wallenkampf, "Emergency Health Impact of a Severe Storm," *American Journal of Emergency Medicine*, Vol. 7, 1989, pp. 598–604.

General Accounting Office, "Report to the Chairman, Subcommittee on VA, HUD, and Independent Agencies, Committee on Appropriations U.S. Senate: Resource Allocation Has Improved, But Better Oversight Is Needed," United States General Accounting Office GAO/HEHS-97-178, September 1997.

General Accounting Office, "Report to the Chairman, Subcommittee on VA, HUD, and Independent Agencies, Committee on Appropriations, U.S. Senate: VA Health Care—Closing a Chicago Hospital Would Save Millions and Enhance Access to Services," United States General Accounting Office GAO/HEHS-98-64, April 1998.

General Accounting Office, "Report to the Secretary of Veterans Affairs: VA Health Care: Improvements Needed in Capital Asset Planning and Budgeting," United States General Accounting Office GAO/HEHS-99-145, August 1999.

Glass, R. I., and M. M. Zack, Jr., "Increase in Deaths from Ischemic Heart Disease After Blizzards," *Lancet*, Vol. 1, 1979, pp. 485–487.

Goldfarb, M. G., and R. M. Coffey, "Case-Mix Differences Between Teaching and Nonteaching Hospitals," *Inquiry*, Vol. 24, Spring 1987, pp. 68–84.

Grannemann, T., R. Brown, and M. Pauly, "Estimating Hospital Costs: A Multiple Output Analysis," *Journal of Health Economics*, Vol. 5, 1986, pp. 107–127.

Hao, S., and C. C. Pegels, "Evaluating Relative Efficiencies of Veterans Affairs Medical Centers Using Data Envelopment, Ratio, and Multiple Regression Analysis," *Journal of Medical Systems*, Vol. 18, No. 2, 1994, pp. 55–67.

Himes, C. L., and T. S. Rutrough, "Differences in the Use of Health Services by Metropolitan and Nonmetropolitan Elderly," *Journal of Rural Health*, Vol. 10, No. 2, 1994, 80–88.

Jones, H. P., and M. K. Brand, "Providing Rehabilitative Services in Rural Communities: Report of a Conference," *Journal of Rural Health*, Vol. 11, No. 2, 1995, pp. 122–127.

Jones, T. S., A. P. Liang, E. M. Kilbourne, M. R. Griffin, P. A. Patriarca, S. G. Wassilak, R. J. Mullan, R. F. Herrick, H. D. Donnell, Jr., K. Choi, and S. B. Thacker, "Morbidity and Mortality Associated with the July 1980 Heat Wave in St. Louis and Kansas City, MO," *Journal of the American Medical Association*, Vol. 247, 1982, pp. 3327–3331.

Journal of the American Medical Association (JAMA), "Graduate Medical Education," *Journal of the American Medical Association*, Vol. 283, No. 9, 2000, Appendix II.

Kalkstein, L. S., "Health and Climate Change: Direct Impact in Cities," *Lancet*, Vol. 342, December 4, 1993, pp. 1397–1399.

Kalkstein, L. S., and R. E. Davis, "Weather and Human Mortality: An Evaluation of Demographic and Interregional Responses in the United States," *Annals of the Association of American Geographers*, Vol. 79, 1989, pp. 44–64.

Kilbourne, E. M, "Illness Due to Thermal Extremes," in R. B. Wallace, ed., *Public Health and Preventive Medicine*, Stanford, Conn.: Appleton & Lange, 1998, pp. 607–617.

Lave, J. R., "The Cost of Graduate Medical Education in Outpatient Settings: A Report of a Study by a Committee of the Institute of Medicine, Division of Health Care Services." Paper commissioned by the Committee to Study Strategies for Financing Graduate Medical Education for Primary Care Physicians in Ambulatory Settings. Washington, D.C.: National Academy Press, 1989, pp. 144–172.

Lehner L. A., and J. F. Burgess, Jr., "Teaching and Hospital Production: The Use of Regression Estimates," *Health Economics*, Vol. 4, 1995, pp. 113–125.

Levitz, G. S., and P. P. Brooke, Jr., "Independent Versus System-Affiliated Hospitals: A Comparative Analysis of Financial Performance, Cost, and Productivity," *Health Services Research*, Vol. 20, No. 3, 1985, pp. 315–339.

Liaison Committee on Medical Education, *Functions and Structure of a Medical School: Standards for Accreditation of Medical Education Programs Leading to the M.D. Degree.* September 1998 with July 1999 supplement.

Longstreth, J., "Public Health Consequences of Global Climate Change in the United States: Some Regions May Suffer Disproportionately," *Environmental Health Perspectives*, Vol. 107, Suppl. 1, February 1999, pp. 169–179.

Luft, H. S., D. W. Garnick, D. H. Mark, and S. J. McPhee, "Hospital Volume, Physician Volume, and Patient Outcomes: Assessing the Evidence," Ann Arbor, Mich.: Health Administration Press, 1990.

Lynk, W. J., "The Creation of Economic Efficiencies in Hospital Mergers," *Journal of Health Economics*, Vol. 14, 1995, pp. 507–530.

Madden, C. W., B. P. Mackay, S. M. Skillman, M. Ciol, and P. K. Diehr, "Risk Adjusting Capitation: Applications in Employed and Disabled Populations," *Health Care Management Sciences*, Vol. 3, 2000, pp. 101–109.

Management Sciences Group, "2000 Diagnostic Cost Group Briefing."

Management Sciences Group, "2001 DCG Risk Adjustment Ranking and VERA Recurring Cost by VISN from FY 1998 Data."

Mechanic, R., K. Coleman, and A. Dobson, "Teaching Hospital Costs Implications for Academic Missions in a Competitive Market," *Journal of the American Medical Association*, Vol. 280, No. 11, 1998, pp. 1015–1019.

Medicare Payment Advisory Commission, "Rethinking Medicare's Payment Policies for Graduate Medical Education and Teaching Hospitals," Washington, D.C., August 1999.

Medicare Payment Advisory Commission, "Report to the Congress: Medicare Payment Policy," Washington, D.C., March 2000.

Mirvis, D. M., L. A. Ingram, A. O. Kilpatrick, and S. Magnetti, "Medical School Affiliations with Department of Veterans Affairs Medical Centers: Attitudes of Medical Center Leadership," *American Journal of Medical Sciences*, Vol. 308, 1994, pp. 162–166.

National Health Policy Forum Issue Brief, "Restructuring the VA Health Care System: Safety Net, Training, and Other Considerations," Washington, D.C., 1998.

Nemet, G. F., and A. J. Bailey, "Distance and Health Care Utilization Among the Rural Elderly," *Social Science & Medicine*, Vol. 50, No. 9, 2000, pp. 1197–1208.

Office of Inspector General, "Summary Report: Audits of VA–Medical School Affiliation Issues," Department of Veterans Affairs OIG Report No. 7R8-A99-026, 1997.

Office of Inspector General, "Evaluation of VA Capital Programming Practices and Initiatives," Department of Veterans Affairs OIG Report No. 8R8-A19-061, 1998.

Patz, J. A., D. Engelberg, and J. Last, "The Effects of Changing Weather on Public Health," *Annual Review of Public Health*, Vol. 21, 2000, pp. 271–307.

Patz, J. A., M. A. McGeehin, S. M. Bernard, K. L. Ebi, P. R. Epstein, A. Grambsch, D. J. Gubler, P. Reiter, I. Romieu, J. B. Rose, J. M. Samet, and J. Trtanj, "The Potential Health Impacts of Climate Variability and Change for the United States: Executive Summary of the Report of the Health Sector of the U.S. National Assessment," *Environmental Health Perspectives*, Vol. 108, No. 4, April 2000, pp. 367–376.

Philibert, I., "Medical Education in Ambulatory Care Settings: An Annotated Bibliography of Selected Works," 2nd ed. Washington, D.C.: Association of American Medical Colleges, March 1999.

Phillips, S. M., "Measuring Teaching Intensity with the Resident-to-Average Daily Census," *Health Care Financing Review*, Vol. 14, No. 2, 1992, pp. 59–67.

Price Waterhouse LLP and The Lewin Group, Inc., "Veterans Equitable Resource Allocation Assessment Final Report," Department of Veterans Affairs Prime Contract No. V101(93)P-1444 Task Order 24, March 1998.

Rice, N., and P. C. Smith, "Capitation and Risk Adjustment in Health Care Financing: An International Progress Report," *The Milbank Quarterly*, Vol. 79, No. 1, 2001, pp. 81–113.

Rice, N., and P. C. Smith, "Capitation and Risk Adjustment in Health Care: Editorial," *Health Care Management Sciences*, Vol. 3, 2000, pp. 73–75.

Rogot, E., and S. J. Padgett, "Associations of Coronary and Stroke Mortality with Temperature and Snowfall in Selected Areas of the United States, 1962–1966," *American Journal of Epidemiology*, Vol. 103, 1976, pp. 565–572.

Rogowski, J. A., and J. P. Newhouse, "Estimating the Indirect Costs of Teaching," *Journal of Health Economics*, Vol. 11, 1992, pp. 153–173.

Schwartz, W. B., and P. L. Joskow, "Duplicated Hospital Facilities: How Much Can We Save by Consolidating Them?" *New England Journal of Medicine*, Vol. 303, No. 25, 1980, pp. 1449–1957.

Semenza, J. C., J. E. McCullough, D. Flanders, M. A. McGeehin, and J. R. Lumpkin, "Excess Hospital Admissions During the July 1995 Heat Wave in Chicago," *American Journal of Preventive Medicine*, Vol. 16, No. 4, 1999, pp. 269–277.

Sheingold, S. H., "Alternatives for Using Multivariate Regression to Adjust Prospective Payment Rates," *Health Care Financing Review*, Vol. 11, No. 3, 1990, pp. 31–41.

Teschke, D. A., "Even the Weather Can Threaten Hospital Finances," *Healthcare Financial Management*, Vol. 43, 1989, pp. 98–99.

Thorpe, K. E., "The Use of Regression Analysis to Determine Hospital Payment: The Case of Medicare's Indirect Teaching Adjustment," *Inquiry*, Vol. 25, 1998, pp. 219–231.

Vita, M. G., "Exploring Hospital Production Relationships with Flexible Functional Forms," *Journal of Health Economics*, Vol. 9, 1990, pp. 1–21.

Vita, M. G., J. Langenfeld, P. Pautler, and L. Miller, "Economic Analysis in Health Care Anti-Trust," *Journal of Contemporary Health Law & Policy*, Vol. 7, 1991, pp. 73–115.

Wainwright, S. H., S. D. Buchanan, M. Mainzer, R. G. Parrish, and T. H. Sinks, "Cardiovascular Mortality: The Hidden Peril of Heat Waves," *Prehospital and Disaster Medicine*, Vol. 14, No. 4, 1999, pp. 222–231.

Welch, W. P., "Do All Teaching Hospitals Deserve an Add-on Payment under the Prospective Payment System?" *Inquiry*, Vol. 24, 1987, pp. 221–232.

Wilson, N. J., and K. W. Kizer, "The VA Health Care System: An Unrecognized National Safety Net," *Health Affairs*, Vol. 16, No. 4, 1997, pp. 200–204.